McSweeney's

MOUNTAIN MAN
DANCE MOVES

Based in San Francisco, McSweeney's publishes books, a monthly magazine called *The Believer,* and two quarterlies—one for short fiction (*McSweeney's*), and one for short films (*Wholphin*). Since 2002, McSweeney's has shared space with 826 Valencia, a non-profit educational center for Bay Area youth, and has helped support its five sister centers in other cities.

www.mcsweeneys.net

MOUNTAIN MAN DANCE MOVES

THE McSWEENEY'S

BOOK OF LISTS

From the Editors of McSweeney's

This book was compiled by John Warner,
Editor of mcsweeneys.net, and Ed Page, Assistant Editor,
with help from Benjamin R. Cohen,
Jordan Bass, and Eli Horowitz.

VINTAGE BOOKS

A DIVISION OF RANDOM HOUSE, INC.

NEW YORK

A VINTAGE BOOKS ORIGINAL, SEPTEMBER 2006

Copyright © 2006 by McSweeney's Publishing LLC

Library of Congress Cataloging-in-Publication Data
Mountain man dance moves : McSweeney's book of lists / from the
editors of McSweeney's.
p.   cm.
1. McSweeney's.   2. American wit and humor.   I. Title.
PN6165.M68 2006
818'.60208—dc22
2006042164

Vintage ISBN-10: 0-307-27720-8
Vintage ISBN-13: 978-0-307-27720-6

www.vintagebooks.com

Printed in the United States of America
10   9   8   7   6   5   4   3   2   1

MOUNTAIN MAN
DANCE MOVES

With Advice for the Tourist in Germany

[Note: Lists are best read first column first, then second column. When a list does not end at the bottom of a page, it will continue on the next page.]

THINGS KOALA BEARS WOULD SAY

by Timothy Weinmann

Yay!

Love me!

Climbing trees is fun!

Let's volunteer at a soup kitchen this Christmas.

My tongue is funny!

Eating leaves is fun!

Will you help me think of something nice we can do for Grandma?

Look, a pouch!

Let's prevent a forest fire!

No, *you're* the cutest ever.

Camus is boring. I find Karl Jaspers's philosophy much more enlightening.

Wheeee!

Let's make cider!

I bet I'll live forever!

FORMER JOBS HELD BY THE GUY YOU ONCE SAW WEARING THAT "PUSSY PATROL" T-SHIRT

by Mike Sacks

Vagina cop

Titty detective

Part-time perineum security guard

Anus temp

Nipple bureaucrat

Executive vice president of technology and worldwide operations for Merrill Lynch

EXACTLY WHAT I MEAN WHEN I SAY MY EX-GIRLFRIEND KRISTIN AND I "WANTED DIFFERENT THINGS FROM LIFE"

by Dan Kennedy

Something I didn't want from life was for us to stay together after she slept with another man in exchange for cocaine.

Something she wanted from life was for us to stay together after she slept with another man in exchange for cocaine.

7 HABITS OF HIGHLY SUCCESSFUL PEOPLE

by Brendon Lloyd

1. Skiing

2. Yachting

3. Snorkeling

4. Golf

5. Polo

6. Dinner parties

7. Shopping

TOURISM SLOGANS THAT FAILED TO SEAL THE DEAL

by Michelle Orange

Kyrgyzstan: Kazakhstan's Mexico

Germany: Let It Go

Venezuela: We Dare You

Cambodia: Nike's Best Kept Secret

It's Worse in Western Samoa

Canada: Turn Left at Greenland

Syria: Come for the Ruins, Stay Because We Confiscated Your Passport

ANECDOTAL LEADS FOR NEWS STORIES REPORTING THE END OF THE WORLD

by Hart Seely

Nine-year-old Joshua Harding didn't plan to miss classes Tuesday at West Monroe Elementary School. Nobody did.

But dismissed were his classes—for good.

After carefully parking his red Toyota Matrix in the lot outside Dick's Sporting Goods, John P. Boyce strode briskly into the West Burlington store.

He was looking for rain gear on a day when rain gear would not be enough.

"The prices are outrageous," said Boyce, fifty-eight, of West Street, as he sifted through brightly colored slickers and tall rubber boots. "Then again, I guess you could say it's a seller's market."

An hour later, it was a nobody's market.

Tamika Carter had dieted all spring to lose twenty-eight pounds in time for the Independence Day weekend. She skipped lunches and jogged each night after returning home from her job at the Pancake Circus.

"I always try to lose weight before summer," the twenty-seven-year-old Sacramento waitress said. "You want to look good on the beach."

But this summer, looking good on the beach would turn out to be far less important than Carter could have imagined.

Mo Bushnell was not happy.
Not happy at all.
With a wheezing gust

from his eighty-four-year-old lungs, the opinionated former Ashtabula steelworker had managed to blow out all the candles on his large chocolate layer cake. But it was abundantly clear that Bushnell's birthday wish would not be coming true.

Not this year.

Not ever.

Though the sign outside Desi's Show Lounge shouted CLOSED FOR GOOD, Andrew Kramer kept pounding on the front door, as if trying to rouse what spirits of romance might still reside within the abandoned South Side disco.

As his knuckles rapped against the empty building, Kramer found himself humming the classic disco oldie "Last Dance" by Donna Summer.

"Last dance," he sang.

"It's the last chance. For lo-ove."

It was the musical sentiment that echoed across Sarasota Tuesday.

Claude D. LaMont grinned as he stepped from the yellow taxi, then turned to hand the driver a crisp $50 bill.

LaMont was returning from the Oneida Indian Casino, where he had just lost every last penny in his bank account. Not only that, he had gambled away his house, his car, and all his earthly possessions.

"Who the heck cares?" LaMont said, flicking his cigarette butt to the curb. "In a matter of hours, we're all dead."

And he was right.

With a broad smile emerging from his salt-and-pepper beard, gas station attendant Earl Talbot hailed the little man in the shiny red Porsche that had pulled up to pump no. 3 and demanded, "Fill 'er up!"

Without skipping a beat, Talbot unveiled the sawed-off shotgun he kept behind his back and blasted four bullets into the unidentified driver's skull. Then, with a tortured howl directed at the sky, Talbot placed the muzzle of the gun in his wide mouth and pulled the trigger.

For the Exit 41 Kwik Fill, the final exit had come.

GOOD LAST LINE TO A SYNDICATED PRISON HUMOR COLUMN

by Mike Sacks

"Anyway, I guess that's why they call it prison."

REJECTED BOND GIRLS

by Rebecca Waits

Chlamydia Johnson

Pussy Notsomuch

Gloria Abortion

Incestua

Plenty O'Hep

Jenny Arthritis

S'phyllis

Star Jones

SIGNS YOUR UNICORN IS CHEATING ON YOU

by Christopher Monks

Seems emotionally distant and uninterested

Wears fancier tail ribbons

Starts working out at the gym

Quickly closes its laptop when you walk into its enchanted den

Credit card bill full of charges to area elf lodges

The "three C's": confrontation, criticism, and complaints

Every time you say the word "magic" it sighs forlornly

Is making a movie with Angelina Jolie

BARTLETT'S FAMILIAR QUOTATIONS

by Martin Bell

"Hi there. John Bartlett."
—John Bartlett

"Reservation should be under
'Bartlett.' That's two T's.
Yes. 'Bart-let-et.' "
—John Bartlett

"Yep, that was me. I'm that
Bartlett."—John Bartlett

"Yes, I'd like another one."
—John Bartlett

". . . and I said, 'Yeah, and
you can "quote" me on it!'
Ha, ha!"—John Bartlett

"Ah, yes, where's your
restroom?"—John Bartlett

"Hey there, my little . . . my
little cowgirl. I'm Jack
Bartlett. Want credit for a
quotation? I don't think
anyone's laid claim to your
phone number yet. Nice.
Just . . . just one second, let

me get a pen."—John
Bartlett

"That's not funny. It's not
funny. Don't ask me what,
you know what. The little
quote fingers. All the
goddamn time. Everything I
say. Just . . . just stop.
Okay?"—John Bartlett

"No, how about *you* please
leave the premises? Huh?
How about *you* don't make a
scene? How about . . . how
about that? Well, fine.
Fucking . . . fine. Don't
touch me! Don't you dare
touch me! Fuck you, you
fucking piece of . . . of fuck.
How's that for a bloody
quotation?"—John Bartlett

"Oh, nice one, honey. Yes.
Clever. That's becoming
quite a familiar quotation in
its own right, isn't it? Maybe
I should just add it to the

next edition. 'Mother was right.' Author: Mrs. Bartlett, world-renowned nag. Year: 1859. Attribution: A short play entitled *Every Goddamn Weekend*."—John Bartlett

"Right. Well, you call him and talk about it. Hey, and when you bring it up, ask him about the 'Bartlett's' on the cover. Singular possessive, mind you. Note where the apostrophe is. Ask him if he thinks you're entitled to half the royalties. Just ask him. I have my hunch, but I'm sure his legal opinion counts for a lot more. Go on, call Stanley. If you need me, I'll be in bed."—John Bartlett

PUNCH LINES THAT WOULD ONLY SEEM FUNNY TO YOU AND THE GUY YOU JUST SPENT THE LAST TEN YEARS WITH IN A PIT

by Mike Sacks

"When the buzzard came down and ate that dead rat's eye."

"The month we couldn't move because we were so weak with hunger."

"The insects."

"The sun that time."

"When the kid peeked over the lip of the hole and then ran off and never came back, he almost slipped and fell in also. The look in his eyes, oh man!"

"Hallucinating for the entirety of 1999 that we were characters in a classic Beach Boys song."

"Let's get serious now. The past ten years have been a hell of a ride, bro. Good times."

THINGS THIS CITY WAS BUILT ON BESIDES ROCK 'N' ROLL

by Eric March

Navajo burial ground

Twelve billion tons of reinforced concrete and steel

Government-protected wetlands

Drunken dare

Waterlogged corpses of Irish immigrants

Previous bizarro underground version of this city

OTHER PLACES JIMMY BUFFETT WASTED AWAY

by Chris Steck

Slipperynippleberg

Jelloshootersdale

Bloodymarysfield

Jägermeisterplatz

Frozendaiquiriland

Cubalibretown

Boilermakerstad

NAMES THAT COULD POSSIBLY PASS FOR CRIES OF PASSION IF ACCIDENTALLY YELLED DURING SEX WITH ANYONE NOT SO NAMED

by Emily Lloyd

Aaliyah

Maura

Ewan

Osgood

Deepak

Uma

Ja Rule

Moe

GERMANY

Travellers entering Germany through one of
the North Sea ports and working their way
down to the snow-clad mountains of Bavaria,
can not fail to be impressed by the infinite
beauty and charm of the ever-shifting panorama.
Here in a space no larger than the state of
Texas, Nature has painted one of her incomparable canvasses. Virgin forests alternate with
fertile fields; high wooded slopes separate ver-
dant valleys; famous old cities are reflected in
historic rivers; and to the traveller who, maybe,
is revisiting the scene after an absence of many
years there rises on the joyous wave of recol-
lection the memory of impressive cathedrals,
priceless art treasures and the inspiring messages
of a Bach, a Beethoven or a Richard Wagner.
Despite the utilitarian trend of the age, Germany is still replete with romance and poetry;
every city is an eloquent chronicler of the old
as well as of the new, and it is the old, the
picturesque, the unique of which people come
in quest when penetrating to the heart of a
foreign country.

NAMES GAS-STATION ATTENDANTS CALL ME THAT LEAVE ME FEELING OVERWHELMED

by Rob Eccles

Chief

Boss

GUIDE TO DETERMINE IF YOU ARE IN A JERRY BRUCKHEIMER MOVIE

by Peter W. Suderman

Your girlfriend is a waitress, but could be a model.

A bus explodes.

A psychopathic millionaire devises an elaborate plan to murder you or someone you know . . .
. . . and you feel compelled to stop it.

You are Nicolas Cage.

Despite a total lack of training, you are able to shoot and fight with the accuracy and ability of a Special Forces soldier.

You are a cop or scientist, but could be a model.

A building explodes.

You are in a shoot-out on the streets of a major city . . .
. . . and it involves helicopters and rocket launchers.

You are engaged in a knock-down, drag-out brawl with the leader of a major crime organization . . .
. . . in slow motion.

Everyone around you is a model.

Everything that has not yet exploded explodes.

Teams of well-trained henchmen are shooting at you, but they all miss.

NOW PLAYING AT THE ZOMBIETOWN 12-SCREEN CINEPLEX

by John Moe

Breakfast of Tiffanys

My Dinner of Andre

Better Off Dead

A Beautiful Mind

Throw Momma from Her Brain

Footloose

Alive (two screens)

Ocean's 11 with the Tops of Their Skulls Removed

ADJECTIVES RARELY USED BY WINE TASTERS

by Adam Koford

Chunky

Supercharged

Pondy

Wine-a-licious

Alcoholy

CURRENT FOOTBALL PLAYERS IF THEY DECIDED TO SPELL THEIR LAST NAME LIKE BRETT FAVRE

by Jason DeLorenzo

Drew Bledose

Ben Reothlibsegrer

Vinny Testavedre

Jerry Rcie

Chris Fuamtau-Ma'alfaa

Michael Vcik

Jamal Leiws

Willis MaGaehe

Laveranues Coels

Brett Farve

CINEMATIC EXPRESSIONS OF INNER SELF-LOATHING IF THERE WERE NO MIRRORS TO SMASH

by Ross Murray

Junkie jazz singer sees self in back of spoon; uses telekinetic powers to bend it until it snaps in two.

Actress who clawed her way to the top catches reflection in pond; uses nearby backhoe to drain pond.

Woman who married for wealth rather than love looks at photo on driver's license; goes to DMV to ask for new photo.

Politician who has forsaken his grassroots values discovers potato in shape of own head; mashes it.

Burned-out rock star looks down at himself during out-of-body experience; refuses to go back in body "until we start seeing some changes around here, mister."

Aging supermodel has plaster cast made of face; backs over it in SUV.

Alcoholic author looks at reflection in a tumbler of Scotch; drinks Scotch; pours another to see if he looks any better in this one.

TWO BUGS ON DISPLAY AT THE MONTREAL INSECTARIUM, THE FIRST OF WHICH I THOUGHT VERY IMPRESSIVE UNTIL I SAW THE SECOND

by Dan Guterman

Centipede

Millipede

ALTERNATIVES TO "OPENING A CAN O' WHUPASS" FOR THE LESS CONFRONTATIONALLY INCLINED

by Ian Carey

Unsnapping a Purse o' Politeness

Sipping a Demitasse o' Diplomacy

Decanting a Carafe o' Contrition

Refrigerating the Tupperware o' Temperance

Unzipping a Fanny Pack o' Friendliness

Unscrewing a Thermos o' Thoughtfulness

Gently Folding a Napkin o' Negotiation	Lightly Greasing a Ramekin o' Retreat
Checking the Date on a Carton o' Caution	Applying a Beechwood Veneer to a Hutch o' Hiding
Serving an Aperitif o' Avoidance	Cleaning out a Drawer o' Disappearance

PROPOSED NICKNAMES FOR THE *TODAY* SHOW'S MATT LAUER

by Dan Kennedy

Mr. Smuggy Pants

Smugly Grinning, Esq.

Smug-o

Rich Smugly, President,
Above It All, Inc.

YOUR RECURRING DREAMS ABOUT UNICORNS EXPLAINED, 1970S BASEBALL EDITION

by Carlton Doby

You have an unresolved financial conflict with former Red Sox pitcher Dick Pole.

You are worried your father will die and your mother will marry former Royals first baseman Pete LaCock.

You are concerned that former Rangers pitcher John Henry Johnson will lose all his teeth.

You are jealous of your father and sister for monopolizing the affections of former Tigers pitcher Woodie Fryman.

You are envious of former Astros third baseman Enos Cabell, although why exactly is unclear.

POPULAR SONGS RENAMED ALONG THE LINES OF THE CATTLEMEN'S BEEF BOARD AD CAMPAIGN "BEEF, IT'S WHAT'S FOR DINNER"

by Geoff Smith

"Me, It's What's for Leaning On"

"Wu-Tang Clan, It's What Ain't Nothing Ta Fuck Wit'"

"Back, It's What Baby Got"

"The House, It's What's Burning Down"

"Alles, It's What California's Über"

"The Street, It's What's for Dancing In"

"Penis, It's What's Detachable"

"Dead, It's What Ed Is"

"The Dust, It's What Another One Bites"

"The Bong, It's What Hits Are From"

"U, It's What I Would Die 4"

"London, It's What's Calling"

"Brooklyn, It's What There's No Sleep Till"

"The Volume, It's What's Pumped Up"

"Bigger, It's What Some Girls Are Than Others"

EXCERPTS FROM AN ACTUAL 1970 VIETNAM-ERA NAVY-RECRUITMENT FILM TARGETING BLACK AMERICANS, NARRATED BY LOU RAWLS

by Angelo Young

"Of course, everybody has
to go through boot camp . . .
you get checked in and you
get threaded out."

"Of course, you have to get
the ol' bod in shape, you
know what I mean? And you
learn to swim—yeah, swim,
man, you dig?"

"And, don't forget, you're
getting paid all the time,
you understand?"

"You don't have to go alone.
The navy has what they call
the buddy system. Where
you and a friend from home
can join the navy together.
And that's a gas."

MY FANTASY SPORTS ROSTERS

by John Moe

Football

QB: Steve McNair
RB: LaDainian Tomlinson
RB: Franco Harris
WR: Legolas
WR: Icarus
WR: Marvin Harrison
TE: Jaclyn Smith with a huge plate of bacon
DEF: Soviet Union, circa 1944
K: Pelé

Basketball

G: Dwyane Wade
G: Aldo Nova
F: A pony
F: Christian Laettner (Duke version only)
C: A 23-foot-compendium of Shawn Bradley, Manute Bol, and Gheorge Muresan

Baseball

1B: Todd Helton
2B: That girl in college who, when I looked back on it, might have been kind of into me
SS: Omar Vizquel
3B: A constantly regenerating pizza
OF: Ichiro Suzuki
OF: God
OF: Kid Rock
C: Thurman Munson living to a ripe old age
LHP: World peace
RHP: I become the lead singer of Led Zeppelin

QUESTIONS FROM THE FBI EMPLOYMENT APPLICATION MEANT TO FILTER OUT UNICORNS DISGUISED AS PEOPLE

by Wendy Molyneux

Would you describe yourself as unicorny?

I have:
    A. One horn in the middle of my head.
    B. No horns.

True or false: I am a unicorn.

LAST NAMES CLEARLY DERIVED FROM ANCESTRAL PROFESSIONS

by Sam Means

Carpenter   Garbagemann

Smith   Baker

Tanner   Secretaryvich

Hooper	Dentisté
Miller	Mason
Barber	Taylor
Editorson	Whoreberg

WHAT TO THINK ABOUT WHEN TWO ADULTS COME AND COMPLAIN TO YOU ABOUT HOW THEY CANNOT GET ALONG WITH EACH OTHER AT WORK

by Dave Best

Being in a spaceship

and no gravity

and coffee

and monkeys

and shit like that.

EXTREME WAYS TO BREAK YOUR ARM

by Rick Stoeckel

Skateboarding

Hand-to-hand combat with Steven Seagal in *Out for Justice*

Mountain climbing

Engage in martial-arts battle with Steven Seagal in *Under Siege*

Gymnastics

Attempt to punch Steven Seagal in *Marked for Death*

Rugby

Run menacingly toward Steven Seagal in *Above the Law*

NECROPHILIAC PICKUP LINES

by Mike DiCenzo

"I'm pretty sure I'm not going to get you pregnant."

"Would you like to have sex? I'll take silence as a yes."

THINGS THIS ONE GIRL SITTING NEAR ME IN A MOVIE THEATER SAID OUT LOUD WHEN ONE OF THE CHARACTERS WAS SHOWN PULLING INTO A GAS STATION

by Conley Wouters

"Oh, he's going to stop for gas."

SEVEN BAND NAMES THAT WOULD BE IMPOSSIBLE TO BOOK

by Mike Hampton

No Event Scheduled

Open Date

Postponed

All Ages w/ No Cover

Renovating

Private Party

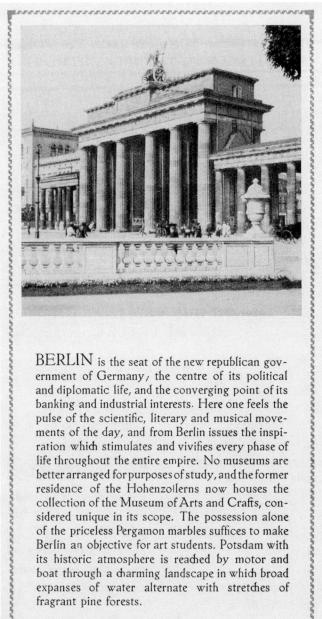

BERLIN is the seat of the new republican government of Germany, the centre of its political and diplomatic life, and the converging point of its banking and industrial interests. Here one feels the pulse of the scientific, literary and musical movements of the day, and from Berlin issues the inspiration which stimulates and vivifies every phase of life throughout the entire empire. No museums are better arranged for purposes of study, and the former residence of the Hohenzollerns now houses the collection of the Museum of Arts and Crafts, considered unique in its scope. The possession alone of the priceless Pergamon marbles suffices to make Berlin an objective for art students. Potsdam with its historic atmosphere is reached by motor and boat through a charming landscape in which broad expanses of water alternate with stretches of fragrant pine forests.

NEW SLOGANS FOR AMERICA TO USE TO SELL ITSELF TO THE ISLAMIC WORLD

by Rob Bates

The Great Satan Is Now Just Plain Great!

The Overwhelming Military Power with a Heart

We're Infidel-ightful!

Standing for Freedom and Democracy a Good Percentage of the Time

TOUCHDOWN CELEBRATIONS OF THE FUTURE

by Peter Haas

Run to local church, convert to Catholicism, then run back to end zone and make the sign of the cross

Write "paragon of athletic achievement" in the air with hand

Shimmy up goalpost, refuse to come back down

Calmly pull football apart at the seams, then carefully place remnants on ground

Dump cooler of Gatorade on self

Enter press box, write article praising my performance

Take out cell phone hidden in padding on goalpost, call up fire department and tell them there's a man on fire at the stadium. Add, "It's me! Get it? *Get it?*"

UNCHARACTERISTICALLY HOMOEROTIC TALK FROM THE TWO STRAITLACED CONSERVATIVE BUSINESSMEN HAVING LUNCH AT THE TABLE NEXT TO MINE

by Dan Kennedy

"I need you to do this if you want to do this, and if you don't that's fine, but you need to figure that out."

"We're the only ones mixing latex and water like this."

"Nobody has been with me from the beginning other than me, so it's my ass."

"This is not a Larry-bashing party."

"This is a very specialized situation."

"Bill's fine."

"I won't throw someone's ass to the dogs."

"If I were in Bill's shoes, I would say to Larry, 'Look . . . we're going to do it this week. Period. And that's that.' "

"We're going to have some long nights ahead of us on this."

"My wife is going to leave me if we don't get this thing finished."

"I need you to understand it's a sensitive situation with Larry."

"Okay, let's do it, then."

REACTIONS I OVERHEARD UPON RIDING A UNICORN INTO MY TEN-YEAR HIGH SCHOOL REUNION

by Mike Sacks

"Guy hasn't changed a bit."

"Mark, right? Wait a second . . . Mitch?"

"Does he really believe that this is going to take away from the fact that he's going bald?"

"Ha! He's riding the same type of unicorn as Ben Devine's, except Ben's is bigger and prettier."

SIX DEGREES OF KEVIN BACON

by Colin Gardner

BA in entomology

BS in communications

MS in cellular biochemistry

Executive MBA in business administration

PhD in veterinary biosciences

PhD in dancing for his life

SEMICRUDE SENSE-BASED IMPERATIVE STATEMENTS TO SWIPE THE DIGNITY OF BIRTHDAY MILESTONES

by Brian McMullen

"Lordy, lordy, look who's forty."

"Shitty, shitty, smell who's fifty."

"Sonofabitchty, listen who's sixty."

"Beventy, beventy, he's seventy but looks older because he worked in a mine."

"Cratey, cratey, let's put the eighty-year-old in a crate or something."

"Something about tasting twenty-year-olds."

GREAT BOOKS OF THE TWENTIETH CENTURY, AS REVIEWED BY MY BOSS

by Nathan Thornton, copywriter

On the Road
by Jack Kerouac:
"Seems forced."

Portnoy's Complaint
by Philip Roth:
"Nobody's going to read all of that."

The Sun Also Rises
by Ernest Hemingway:
"This feels like Macy's to me."

To the Lighthouse
by Virginia Woolf:
"It needs to be like, New York. It needs to have that energy."

Invisible Man
by Ralph Ellison:
"This isn't like what we talked about."

Ulysses
by James Joyce:
"That's a lot of copy."

The Great Gatsby
by F. Scott Fitzgerald:
"It's a step in the right direction, but it needs to say 'sexy' or 'new.' "

Lolita by Vladimir Nabokov:
"There's no way it can be
that long."

The Adventures of Augie March
by Saul Bellow:
"It's not about what the

words are, it's about the type
treatment and the images."

The Sound and the Fury
by William Faulkner:
"This needs to be about half
as long."

EIGHT REASONS WHY A TYRANNOSAUR CAUGHT IN A TORNADO IS A FUNNY THING TO THINK ABOUT

by Austin Allen

1. The tiny, flailing arms

2. The helpless
"RARRRRRR!"

3. The angry, wild-eyed
expression

4. That dinosaur with the
sail on his back floats by and
he's just cruisin'

5. The landing

6. The *Wizard of Oz* music
playing in the background.
What an anachronism!

7. Tyrannosaurs inhabited
the western United States,
an area of the country known
for its heavy tornado activity.
Statistically speaking, it is
probable that the scenario in
question actually happened
at least once. In this, as in all
enduring comedy, there is a

grain of indubitable truth
inside the humor.

8. "RARRRRRR!" Ha-ha-ha-
ha-ha! "RAAAARRRRRR
RRRR!"

CIRCUMSTANCES UNDER WHICH
A $4 UMBRELLA WILL BREAK

by Geoff Haggerty

Heavy wind   Sleet

Moderate wind   Rain

Wind   If you touch it

Snow

OTHER WARNING LIGHTS THAT MY NEW CAR SHOULD HAVE, CONSIDERING THE FREQUENCY WITH WHICH IT DEMANDS THAT I PUT NEW AIR IN ITS TIRES

by Beth Edwards

There's a piece of lint on me.

Don't drive through that mud puddle!

I'm going to honk at him just for fun.

It's kind of chilly out here, don't you think?

Deodorize me!

Do you think I'd look pretty in red?

I'm just a hair too close to that other car for my comfort level.

How come you never take me on a drive through the mountains, like that car in the commercial?

I'm bored.

I wish I were getting washed by $6.50-an-hour Latino guys in red jumpsuits.

JESUS'S BAR MITZVAH SPEECH: TALKING POINTS

by Mike Sacks

Thanks for coming.

Helped some lepers on the way back from school once.

No longer a boy anymore, but now a son of God or something something.

Faced with a choice: could either go straight to heaven or I could stay down here and study for the bar mitzvah. I think I chose wisely.

I've performed a lot of miracles in my short life, but I think the most miraculous was that I actually finished writing this personal speech! (Wait for laugh.)

Sure, I enjoy turning water into wine, but guess what? I'm not yet old enough to drink it, so what's the big whoop? (Wait for laugh.)

I'd like to thank everybody for coming today and I do hope you all enjoy the party. The theme, by the way, is Dungeons & Dragons.

ACTIVITIES THAT MUST HAVE OCCURRED IN ORDER TO PRODUCE A PEPTO-BISMOL COMMERCIAL FEATURING DANCE MOVES BASED ON GASTROINTESTINAL AILMENTS

by Lars Ostrom

An ad agency developed ten concepts, representing fifty hours of billable time. Each creator made an impassioned pitch to the team, strenuously advocating for his or her idea. Deep discussion and argument followed.

Seven of these ideas were discarded due to substandard quality, off-target messaging, or impractical production demands.

Three concepts were presented to marketing executives at Procter & Gamble in a plush boardroom with leather chairs and tasteful lighting. Detailed storyboards for each concept were unveiled, one by one, as the collective anticipation in the room reached a satisfying crescendo.

Two concepts were deemed inferior to the "dance moves" idea. P&G marketing executives praised its physical manifestations of nausea, heartburn, indigestion, upset stomach, and diarrhea—not to mention its playful homage to the macarena.

Staff writers produced multiple drafts of a shooting script. During weeks of revisions, P&G marketing executives suggested improvements, additions, and tweaks, which the writers dutifully incorporated into the final approved version.

Actors auditioned for each of the five roles. Auditions required the actors to perform impromptu interpretive dances inspired by bodily discomfort.

Most of the actors did not receive callbacks and were gravely disappointed. "Fuck, man," one said to his roommate. "I didn't get the Pepto thing." Some of the actors fired their agents. Others sank deeper into downward spirals of self-loathing and addiction.

Five actors were cast. One of them called her mother, exclaiming: "I'm the diarrhea girl! I'm the diarrhea girl!"

A choreographer helped the actors learn the individual moves for each ailment, then combined the moves into a single, fluid expression of modern dance. One of the actors kept getting the hand motions for upset stomach and indigestion confused. "Remember! UP-set stomach is UP here!" the choreographer urged. "Indigestion is DOWN. Let's take it from the top."

A paid professional film crew captured multiple takes of the actors dancing with abandon. The director coaxed the best performance from each of them. Everyone broke for lunch, then returned to filming later in the afternoon.

They repeated this process the next day.

The best takes were assembled into the final thirty-second version, which was labored over intensely during postproduction.

The ad agency was told to "keep up the good work."

P&G paid more than one million dollars to broadcast the commercial during prime time in thirty major markets across the United States.

The ad agency's B team was later recruited to create an interactive version of the commercial as a centerpiece of www.pepto-bismol.com.

WHAT MAKES UNICORNS CRY?

by Bob Shea

Seasonal allergies

Those who refuse to believe in them

Orphans throwing rocks at them

Renegade wizards who refuse to join the alliance

A sad movie

Getting punched in the horn

Unicorn-themed fan fiction

War, poverty, injustice— same stuff as you and me

Older, mean-spirited unicorns

Your habitual lying

Overactive thyroid

A LITERARY EXPERIMENT! MORE SPECIFICALLY, THE OPENING LINE TO A SHORT STORY ABOUT AN ADORABLE YELLOW ZEBRA NAMED QUILTY, WRITTEN ENTIRELY WITHOUT THE LETTERS "Z," "Y," OR "Q"

by Mike Sacks

Once there lived an animal that was not 100 percent white and not 100 percent green, but was somewhere right in between. This animal was not a rabbit and not a horse, but it did have stripes. He was a bit old-fashioned and just a bit strange. He was an adorable ellow ebra with the name of uilt.

THE MOST BEAUTIFUL MEN IN THE WORLD

by Runjit Chandra

Me	The guy writing this list
Myself	A clone of me
I	A clone of the clone of me
That guy on my driver's license	Orlando Bloom . . . playing me
The guy in my mirror	

WAYS I WOULD SUBTLY MENTION MY RECENT INVENTION OF THE HOVERBOARD IN EVERYDAY CONVERSATION

by Jonathan Rein

"Yeah, traffic was terrible yesterday. Well, not for me, since I soared above it on my hoverboard."

"I like your hat. I would get one like it, but I'd probably lose it while riding my hoverboard."

"Yes, this week has gone by fast—fast like the hoverboard I invented."

"Excuse me. Could you pick up my pen? Unfortunately, it is susceptible to gravity, unlike my hoverboard."

"Did someone say 'hoverboard'? No? Well, now that we're on the subject . . ."

"Hoverboard! Which I invented."

BREMEN so the uninitiated might be inclined
to think, is like every other port merely a point of
ingress and engress. But this feeling is dispelled
from the moment the incoming traveller finds himself standing in the chief square surrounded by the
most impressive monuments of medieval architecture to be found in all Germany. Here is the Town
Hall with its famous winding staircase dating from
the golden period of the German Renaissance; the
Merchant's Exchange with its fine old Guild Hall;
the eight hundred year old Cathedral; and as an
impressive reminder of Bremen's early history, the
awe-inspiring Roland Statue, betokening the municipal freedom granted to this member of the trinity
of old Hanseatic cities. If you have travelled by a
North-German Lloyd boat you will be interested
in the magnificent building housing this far-flung
shipping line.

THE NAMES OF THE PRESIDENT, THE VICE PRESIDENT, THE CHIEF OF STAFF, AND THE MEMBERS OF THE PRESIDENTIAL CABINET ACCORDING TO THE ETYMOLOGICAL BACKGROUNDS OF THEIR FIRST AND LAST NAMES AND THEIR MIDDLE NAMES WHEN AVAILABLE*

by Jørgen G. Cleemann

The earthworker who engages in the practice of shrinking and thickening wool and dwells near the thicket, President

The brave power who hails from the oak forest around the French town of Brieuse, Vice President

The manly one who prepares wool for spinning and weaving and lives near a mound, White House Chief of Staff

The bright nobleman who is son of the battlemaker, Attorney General

The fierce warrior with sweetness, Secretary of State

The ruler of the world and the ruler of the home who hails from the field of wild garlic, Secretary of Defense

The wellborn warrior who regularly invokes the name of God, Secretary of Agriculture

---

* Secretary of Transportation Norman Yoshio Mineta omitted due to unavailability of reliable translation.

The warrior who descends
from the ruler of the army,
Secretary of Commerce

The little pearl-encrusted
scythe, Secretary of
Education

The bathhouse builder who
has been heard by God,
Secretary of Energy

The pious and humble man
from the beloved gate that
lies in the land of many
yokes, Secretary of Health
and Human Services

The pious and humble man
who is descended from the
devil, Secretary of Homeland
Security

The battle-ready man who is
descended from one who
believes in the grace of God,
Secretary of Housing and
Urban Development

The graceful tempest from
the northern settlement,
Secretary of the Interior

The torch from the orchid
nest, Secretary of Labor

The exceptionally pale and
pious man who has a desire
to protect, Secretary of the
Treasury

The bright and famous
supplanter who is descended
from he who represents
the victory of the people,
Secretary of Veterans
Affairs

WORDS BEETLE BAILEY'S SARGE WASN'T ALLOWED TO HEAR AS A SMALL BOY

by Joe Randazzo

Ampersand

Asterisk

Percent

Exclamation point

Pound sign

Dollar sign

Vagina

ACTUAL ENGLISH NAMES CHOSEN BY OUR KOREAN ESL STUDENTS IN SUZHOU, CHINA

by Rusty Lee, Liz O'Grady, Dan Schneider, and Gareth Morris

Napoleon

Beyoncé

Whiskey

Virus

Bob Shop

GAMES YOU CAN PLAY WITH A UNICORN

by Ed Page

Hide-and-seek

Ringtoss

WHO'S WHO IN
ARDUOUSLY STRANGE NAMES

by Mike Sacks

Johnny Ouchy

Tom R. Finklepotter

Jimmy Slurps

Otis Aw Shit

Boner von Barrett, Shy Guy

PEOPLE, PLACES, PHRASES, AND EVENTS WHICH, DESPITE THE PROMISE I MADE IN MY NINTH GRADE YEARBOOK TO "ALWAYS REMEMBA," I NOW HAVE NO RECOLLECTION OF WHATSOEVER

by Kristen Roupenian

Prom Hockey Xpress

"Get off my ski!"

Canoe trip in NH with
Karen and PJ

"You got the vibes?"

Silly string wars in the Drew
Mobile

AR, DJ, EM, MT, KN, CK,
CL, RM

Hayley I love you girl!

All the great times I had
with my teachers, family, and
friends at Santa Rosa Junior
High

IF YOSEMITE SAM'S CURSES WERE CONSIDERED REAL PROFANITY AND WERE DUBBED OVER FOR TELEVISION IN THE SAME CLUMSY, UNCONVINCING MANNER AS 1980S R-RATED MOVIES

by Martin Bell

Original version: Get outta there, you rassa-frassin' fur-bearin' critter!
Censored version: Get outta there, you wrestle-freezing, forbearing creature!

Original: Ya no-account, bushwhackin' barracuda!
Censored: Ya NorCal, tush-spankin' barracuda!

Original: Great horny toads! I done dug myself all the way to Chinee!
Censored: Great happy toads! I done dug myself all the way to . . . Is this Asia?

Original: Cut the cards. Not that way, you idjet!
Censored: Cut the cards. Not that way, you widget!

Original: Now, ya racka-frackin' carrot-chewin' varmint! Get a-goin'!
Censored: Now, ya really freaky parrot-screwin' charmer! Get a-goin'!
Recensored: Now, ya rack of funky garrote-spewin' varnish! Get a-goin'!

Original: Listen here, galoot! I'm the rootinest, tootinest here outlaw in the West!
Censored: Listen here! *Salaud!* I'm the fresh 'n' fruitiest here outlaw in the West!

Original: If they make me jump off that diving board one more motherfuckin' time, I swear to God. . . .
How many takes could they possibly need?

Censored: Ooooooooooooh,
I HATES rabbits!

Original: Consarn it!
Censored: Daaaaaayum!

INAPPROPRIATE NAMES
FOR SPECIALTY FURNITURE SHOPS

by Mike Ward

Stool Samples

The Ottoman Empire

Knobs

Hidden In-desk-retion

Great (One) Nightstands

Getting the Chair

STATE SONGS, IF THEY ALL
SUGGESTED THE APATHY OF IDAHO'S
"HERE WE HAVE IDAHO"

by Craig Robertson

"Check It Out, Dude, I
Think That's Florida"

"Well, If You Insist, Then I
Guess I'll Take Indiana"

"Hey, Is That Oregon? Oh, My Mistake. It's Washington"

"Hey, Kentucky, How You Doin'?"

"Texas, Does This Mole Look Irregular to You?"

"I Was Only Born in Arizona, Then We Moved When I was Two"

"No, This Is the Other Carolina, but It's an Honest Mistake"

"Please Pass the Salt, Wyoming"

"What Are You Going to Do, It's Michigan, You Know?"

"Another Day, Another Delaware"

"Do You Like Nevada? If So, Check This Box"

ED HARRELSON, TEEN-DRIVER'S-EDUCATION INSTRUCTOR

by Sean Carman

Hungover most mornings

Responsible for pressing passenger-side brake pedal if situation warrants

Falls asleep during ritual showing of drunk-driving-carnage films

Goes to the trouble of looking back along with student during parallel-parking exercise

Has seen it all

Resists temptation to flirt too overtly with attractive female students

Can be lulled into telling Vietnam War stories to

students who have won his trust

Can be found most Sunday afternoons at the Fireside Lounge

On-again, off-again relationship with Vera, dancer at the Torchlight

Dreams of returning to LA

Drives to forget

LEAST ONOMATOPOETIC VERBS

by Mike Ward

Profiteer

Indoctrinate

Cavort

Hyperextend

Expectorate

Prioritize

Calcify

Incense

Persist

Decimate

POKER TERMINOLOGY I FEEL I COULD GET AWAY WITH USING IF I EVER PLAYED A TOURNAMENT

by Andy Sutherland

"He's holding Babraham Lincolns."

"Lay it down on 'The Tarpits.' "

"Short-weeding the double-down avocado splitter."

"Deuce trips."

"So I pull trash from the flop and end up sinking the *Titanic.*"

"Laboratory rats to the left, and I know the guy on the right has a suicide johnny—nothing else to do but drop the transmission."

"He was short stacked, so I raised with nothing but a bumpy melinda and a bullet."

"Crunking the small blind."

"So a Madeleine Albright pops up on Fourth Street."

"After his raise, I know he's sporting two mustaches, and I can see one otter swimming the river on the flop."

"I've got leaky quads, and I call, after he bulldozes the pit with half his gold towers. I fold."

THINGS HAGRID THE HALF GIANT WOULD SAY IF HE SERVED JESUS INSTEAD OF HARRY POTTER

by Hart Seely

"Blimey, Jeez, it's be gettin' ter lunchtime, an' I could eat meself the back end of a Phil'stine. How 'bout doublin' up a quick pile o' loaves?"

"Budge up, yeh money-changin' lumps! This 'ere boy weren't meant ter be a blinkin' Muggle! Fer gawd sake, he's King o' the Jews!"

"Codswallop! All 'm sayin', boy, is tha' yeh gots ta be eyeballin' tha' Judas bloke. When a disciple goes o'er to the dark side, they's nothin' tha' matters to 'em anymore!"

"Speakin' of cups runnethin' over, laddie, mine's be gettin' a mite dry. How 'bout changin' this 'ere water into somethin' a bit more, well, frisky?"

"Lilies o' the field? What lilies? The way yeh jabber on, yeh all mus' be pullin' straight A's in Professor Dumbledore's Exposit'ry Metaphors and Parables class!"

"Why, if a fellow wanted ta get away clean, Peter-me-lad, all they'd have ter do would be ta deny they ever even knowed Jesus. Uh-oh. I shouldn't eh told yeh that."

"Ah, go boil yer spleen, Pilate! Yeh stink-handed prune! Yeh've done me savior wrong, an' now yeh've gots ter pay!"

BAD NAMES FOR MURDER MYSTERIES

by Kevin Thoreson

It Was Me

The Butler Really Did It. No Joke

Big Tobacco

It Was Suicide, Actually

Think Every Agatha Christie Novel, Only with Squirrels

Larry

DIRECTORS' COMMENTARIES FROM MY DVD COLLECTION

by John Mancini

"This is great."

"This is really powerful."

"I like the way I lit this."

"I wanted to say something about that, but we'll have to move on."

"Sometimes I'd just forget to yell 'Cut.'"

"I love this."

"This was my idea."

"I was a big fan of European film."

"It's like a Wagnerian opera."

"It's almost Shakespearean."

"It's like being in a really good jazz band."

"One thing I wouldn't let go of was the editing."

"I met him at a party."

"Did I mention I kept that jacket?"

"You get a really interesting performance out of people when you introduce a live animal to a scene."

FIVE SIGNS THAT YOUR CHILD MAY BE USING UNICORNS

by Dan Kennedy

Confused and sleepy one minute, enchanted and magical the next

Refers to separate groups of friends as "my old friends" and "my unicorn friends"

Wears T-shirts with slogans referring to "horns" and "spells" and pictures of smallish flying pony-type creatures

Other names for unicorns derived from Greek and Chinese mythology you may hear your child or his/her friends mention: Chio-Tuan, Magic Horse, wild ass, Mary Jane, blow, ecstasy, Thai stick

Argues with teachers about whether or not some types of horselike creatures can fly

Newfound interest in prancing

CHAPTER TITLES FROM MY CREATIONIST TEXTBOOK

by David Ng

Thursday	Wednesday
Saturday	Monday
Embryos	Thermodynamics
Friday	Tuesday
Homosexuality	Candle Making

TOTALITARIAN INSTITUTIONS THAT WOULD HAVE BEEN MORE FITTING FOR GEORGE ORWELL'S *1984*, CONSIDERING HOW THAT YEAR TURNED OUT

by Patrick Cassels

The Ministry of Denim

The Ministry of *Footloose* Starring Kevin Bacon

The Ministry of the Beef and Where It Currently Is

The Ministry of Girls Just Wanting to Have Fun

The Ministry of Fools, and
the Pity with Which Mr. T
Regards Them

KLINGON FAIRY TALES

by Mike Richardson–Bryan

"Goldilocks Dies with Honor
at the Hands of the Three
Bears"

"Snow White and the Six
Dwarves She Killed with
Her Bare Hands and the
Seventh Dwarf She Let Get
Away as a Warning to
Others"

"There Was an Old Woman
Who Lived in a Shoe with a
Big Spike on It"

"The Three Little Pigs Build
an Improvised Explosive
Device and Deal with That
Damned Wolf Once and for
All"

"Jack and the Giant Settle
Their Differences with
Flaming Knives"

"Old Mother Hubbard,
Lacking the Means to
Support Herself with Honor,
Sets Her Disruptor on Self-
destruct and Waits for the
Inevitable"

"Mary Had a Little Lamb. It
Was Delicious"

"Little Red Riding Hood
Strays into the Neutral Zone
and Is Never Heard from
Again, Although There Are
Rumors . . . Awful, Awful
Rumors"

"Hansel and Gretel Offend Vlad the Impaler"

"The Hare Foolishly Lowers His Guard and Is Devastated by the Tortoise, Whose Prowess in Battle Attracts Many Desirable Mates"

ORGANIZATIONS THAT AREN'T SPY AGENCIES

by Mike Ward

FBH (British Herpetologist Federation)

Alpha Omega (international Jewish dentists fraternity)

MI8 (small company that provides support for Microsoft Exchange software)

CIAA (collegiate athletic conference for historically African-American colleges)

Interpal (Palestinian charity)

COLOGNE A story is told of an American traveller who went to Cologne, drank in the beauty of
the incomparable Cathedral, studied its gracious ar-
ches, its stone traceries, its heaven-piercing towers
from every angle, and then turned about and went
back home, saying that he did not wish to have this
impression effaced by further sightseeing. This,
however, was to do scant justice to the other
beauties of the old city. There are the churches
saturated in legendary lore, the interesting street
life, the graceful bridges thrown across the Rhine,
and the ever-shifting picture of the river traffic.
From one of the far-flung towers of the Cathedral
an incomparable panorama of the Rhine with its
castles and vineyards unrolls itself on a clear day.

ACTS PROHIBITED BY THE U.S. HOUSE OF REPRESENTATIVES' PROPOSED FLAG-BURNING AMENDMENT

by James Erwin

Burning the flag

Staring at the flag's cleavage

Assuring the flag that you consider it a really good friend, and then pressuring it to sleep with you

Sullenly agreeing to meet the flag at the coffee shop and staring into your coffee without talking

Cutting off the flag's pleading questions by yelling, "Get a life!"

Calling the flag's best friend at three in the morning to talk about how the flag doesn't understand you

Coming within one hundred yards of the flag in violation of the restraining order

LESSER-KNOWN MOVIE PREQUELS

by Sarah Garb

Borderline-Inappropriate Dancing

Four Bachelorette Parties and a Friend in the Hospital

Joseph and the Nondescript Monochrome Sportcoat

There Are Plenty of Mohicans

PROTECTIVE PROPERTIES OF FRUIT

by Mike Ward

An apple a day keeps the doctor away.

An orange a week keeps your nicotine addiction weak.

A strawberry an hour keeps the Saudi government in power.

A mango a year keeps you from seeing *King Lear.*

A pomegranate a minute keeps the Cubs from winnin' it.

A cherry a millennium keeps average factory wages at a minimum.

A grape a nanosecond keeps the world from understanding the true meaning of the Doors' song "The End."

A canteloupe a century keeps it illegal for you to indenture me.

A raspberry a month keeps right-thinking parents from naming their daughters Ronth.

THINGS MY BOSS SAID TO ME WITHOUT ELABORATING

by Isaiah Dufort

"Quick. Tell me everything of consequence that has happened."

"Sometimes people have to kill themselves, and it's not easy."

"You see? We can make the class system work for us!"

"Well, that's not how I spell your name."

"That's not how to subjugate yourself."

"That woman just honked at me. Do you think she's a lesbian?"

"This isn't civilized."

"We will all be undone in the end."

"That's the problem with the working class. They have no concept of work."

"Did I say that? That's terribly clever."

TWELVE SEQUELS TO *DANCES WITH WOLVES* THAT, DUE TO MONETARY CONSTRAINTS, WERE NEVER PRODUCED

by Eric Feezell

Buys Drinks for Wolves

Makes Sweet Love to Wolves

Eschews the Calls of Wolves

Goes Nearly a Year Without Seeing Wolves

Runs into at Safeway and Has Some Explaining to Do to Wolves

Shrewdly Offers Extra Ticket to See Los Lobos at the Fillmore to Wolves

Once Again, Dances With Wolves

Begins to Seriously See Wolves

Hastily Weds Wolves

Is Repeatedly Untrue to Wolves (NC-17)

Pays Motherfucking Alimony to Wolves

Gets Sloppy, in a Subconsciously Purposeful Gesture, and Is Discovered by Wolves

NICKNAMES FOR TOUGH UNICORNS

by John Moe

Rod

Impaler

Mythdemeanor

Punkture Wound

Horny D

Shaft

Rainblow

Spear-It

Slanted and Enchanted

Drill Bitch

Crazy Horse

UniKorn

UNHELPFUL CLUES GIVEN BY JAN-MICHAEL VINCENT DURING AN OCTOBER 1983 TAPING OF *THE NEW $25,000 PYRAMID* WHERE THE CATEGORY TO BE GUESSED WAS "THINGS YOU DO AT A PARTY"

by Aaron Starmer

Victoria Principal

Little of this, little of that

The neutron dance

Crack wise with Bruce Boxleitner

Whatever floats your
boat, man

Smoke in the pool

That chick that plays
Thelma on *Good Times*

FUTURE WINNERS OF THE *NEW YORKER* CARTOON CAPTION CONTEST

by Roy Futterman

"You are doing something
unusual, Harold!"

"I certainly am in a bar with
other businessmen."

"This desert island is a
bummer."

"I love being wealthy in the
Hamptons."

"I'm saying a cliché in a
different context, Pam."

"I like intercourse."

"I'm thinking something
incongruous to what I'm
doing."

THINGS NOT OVERHEARD AT A CONCEPTUAL ART GALLERY OPENING

by Jason Persse

"White wine, red wine. Who do I have to fuck to get a Capri Sun around here?"

"Let me get this straight— the artist is gay *and* German? You just blew my mind."

"Now that you mention it, I have no idea who designed this shirt."

"I can't. I have to work tomorrow."

"Well, that's obvious, but what do the other three midgets represent?"

ALTERNATIVE ENDINGS TO THE CAPITAL ONE ADS WHERE THE PILLAGING HUNS COME AFTER SOMEONE THEY THINK IS USING A CREDIT CARD THAT IS NOT CAPITAL ONE

by Mike Ward

As the Huns are getting closer, the guy at the cash register says, "Well, I'll just use my Capital One card" and takes out his wallet. But he can't find the card. The

Huns get closer. The guy keeps looking, starting to seem a little worried. The Huns get closer. He's searching his pockets, his jacket, everywhere, but he can't find it! He screams just before the Huns arrive and slice him to pieces. Then one of them looks at the camera and says: "Capital One. Make sure it's in your wallet."

The Huns are sprinting full tilt through the mall toward a woman who's making a credit card purchase of perfume in a department store. The woman looks at the cards in her wallet. We see a Capital One card, a Visa card, and a MasterCard. The Huns get closer. She pulls out a MasterCard. The Huns get closer. Suddenly, from the other side of the mall, a huge wave of fierce-looking warriors comes barreling toward the woman. The Huns are just about to arrive, but the other group gets to her first, passes her, and

starts fighting with the Huns. After a few seconds, the second, larger group has completely and obviously destroyed the Huns. Voice-over: "Having a huge army of Mongols at your side? Priceless. Some things money can't buy. For everything else, there's MasterCard." Fade to black screen with MasterCard logo.

The Huns are barreling toward the apparently incorrect card user. In the process, they run completely over a large, white duck. They arrive at their intended target, and one knocks him over the head with a club. As he falls to the ground, a Capital One card falls out of his hand. The Huns look sheepish and embarrassed. One says, "Gee, do you think he's hurt badly?" The other responds, "I hope he's got that supplemental insurance." The first asks, "What supplemental insurance?" Camera cuts back to squashed duck,

which is silent. The Aflac
logo appears on the screen.

As the Huns are running
through the mall toward the
man who has just announced
his intention to make a
purchase with a non–Capital
One credit card, they run by
an Old Navy store and come
to a screeching halt. They all
take off their armor and
battle gear to reveal a
collection of delightful
mauve and seafoam scarves,
light turquoise zipper-neck
sweaters, and ultra-pleated
pants. Suddenly, they break
into the song "Stuck in the
Middle with You," singing
in a playful singsongy kind
of way. One is licking a giant
lollipop. The song ends.
Voice-over: "New Old Navy
ultra-pleated pants. What's
your wallet in?"

The Huns are rampaging
toward the non–Capital One
card user. They reach him,
but then they keep going
and just continue their
seemingly random pillaging
and destruction. Voice-over:
"Viagra is not for everyone.
Side effects may include
nausea, dizziness, and an
irresistible urge to dress up
like a Hun and wantonly
pillage. Make sure to consult
your doctor."

The Huns are on their
destructive sprint, but
they're not running toward
the non–Capital One user.
Instead, they're running
toward David Spade, who
yells "No!" as they reach him
and finish him off.

THINGS THAT, IF KNOWING IS HALF THE BATTLE, MIGHT BE THE OTHER HALF

by Nico Vreeland

Pretending not to notice

Reporting your opinion instead

Betting on the other guy

Finally letting yourself die

Blackmail

Telling every single person you meet

25 percent drinking, 25 percent weeping

Battling

TOP THREE THINGS Q*BERT IS PISSED ABOUT TODAY

by Mike Singer

1. #@*!&%$!

2. @!#?@!

3. &%#@!&#$

ACTUAL EXAMPLES OF MODEL CONVERSATIONAL PHRASES THAT THE TRAVEL GUIDE *LES ETATS-UNIS DANS VOTRE POCHE: EDITION BILINGUE* (HAITER, 1980) FELT WERE SO CENTRAL TO THE EXPERIENCES LIKELY TO BE UNDERGONE BY FRENCH VISITORS TO AMERICA THAT IT INCLUDED THEM ON ITS COMPANION STUDY CASSETTE TAPE

by Beth Maynard

"It's enough to make you sick."

"But these jumbo jets are quite comfortable."

"To put it in a nutshell, you can't escape the fact that you're a product of capitalist culture."

"Well, crash pads are kinds of very cheap hostels, or rather shelters where you can spend the night for 25 or 50 cents, sometimes for no charge at all."

"Yeah! I'll bet if you laid those burgers end to end they would reach to the moon. Let's go try one, shall we?"

"Are you alluding to the multinational corporations?"

"Where's the fine democratic American melting pot?"

"Better keep our strength to investigate some of those famous Kentucky bourbons they serve around here."

"Mobile home living has really come a long way."

"Hello! We're visitors in Chicago, and we were

THE McSWEENEY'S BOOK OF LISTS

noticing all these security precautions you take to protect your store. Is all this really necessary?"

"If you really want to help us, Jim, let us manage our own affairs."

"All right, wage slave, don't get mad! Get back to your toil before they sack you for goldbricking!"

"I found your great optimism, your vision of a rosy future, to be encouraging and, shall I say, 'seductively' infectious. But I also expect that you and I have different eyeglasses when we look at the current world economy crisis."

"That's not expensive, honey, that's Dream Whip."

"It's no secret that the CIA operates in South America mostly to protect American business interests. Witness that ugly disclosure, some time back, that the CIA helped overthrow President Allende in Chile to prevent nationalization of more U.S. firms there."

"I never dreamed they were so religious here."

"Hey, let's change the channel."

DRESDEN to the mind of the average traveller, means the shrine in which is treasured the marvellous image Raphael made of the Sistine Madonna, the crowning glory of the Dresden Museum. This alone would suffice to invest any city with world fame, but there is still to be considered the scenic charm of the surrounding landscape, the bewildering splendor of the Green Vault, in which August the Strong stored away his unique collections of jewels and precious stones, of crystal and ivory, of enamels and bronzes, of the historic old Opera House which Germany's great composer, Richard Strauss has chosen as the scene of all his "first-nights!" A sojourn in Dresden also embraces a visit to "Saxon Switzerland" most justly called and to the quaint old city of Meissen, the home of the porcelain which forms one of the pinnacles of German artistic achievement.

DISCARDED TITLES FOR TONI BRAXTON'S 1996 HIT "UN-BREAK MY HEART"

by Thomas Desmond

"Unforget My PIN"

"Unstain My Rug"

"Unrunover My Dog"

"Undent My Car"

"Unbounce My Check"

"Unwatch My *Blues Brothers 2000*"

ERRORS IN COMMUNICATION BETWEEN MY HAIRDRESSER AND ME IN THE FORM OF WHAT I SAID AND WHAT HE HEARD

by Jez Burrows

Said: Just a little off the length, and a little thinned out?
Heard: Could you make me look like a clown's apprentice?

Said: A little shorter, thanks.
Heard: I want the style that would emerge if you combined all three of Charlie's Angels.

Said: Just the usual—little shorter and thinner.
Heard: You know when you have a bubble bath and you shape the bubbles all around your head? I want it like that.

Said: If you could take some of the width off, that'd be great.

Heard: If you could make it hard for me to appear in public, that'd be great.

Said: Of course it isn't okay—you've disfigured me beyond repair. I look like a mushroom.
Heard: That's perfect. Take my money.

PICKUP LINES: THE FIRST DRAFTS

by Mark Vanderhoff

"Are your legs tired? Oh, well, I'm not surprised; your thighs are almost comically muscular."

"You must wash your pants with Windex, because something really smells like Windex."

"Your father must have been a thief. I don't know, you just have the look of someone who was raised by criminals."

"If I said you had a beautiful body, would you hold it against me? That is to say, would you be offended by my comment, not would you physically hold your body against mine. Sorry for any confusion. Anyways, would you?"

"Do you have a little Italian in you? Really? Wait, what was your last name again? Oh, yeah, I guess that does sound Irish. Never mind."

"If I could rearrange the alphabet, I probably wouldn't. Can you imagine how much that would screw with everybody?"

"Are you from Tennessee? I hate people from Tennessee."

"Excuse me; I seem to have misplaced my inmate number, which was assigned to me by this state's accursed penal system after it was discovered that I was indeed the Fruit-by-the-Foot Strangler. Can I borrow yours?"

"Can I borrow a quarter? I need to call my mother and tell her I've found the girl I'm going to annoy for the next five to ten minutes."

WHY YOU SHOULD NOT RELY ON A UNICORN TO MANAGE YOUR INVESTMENT PORTFOLIO

by Sean Carman

Too busy polishing horn to read quarterly reports or keep up with business pages

Too busy batting eyelashes to understand your long-term investment goals

Tends to believe the most
optimistic quarterly earnings
projections

Keeps files in an enchanted
tree

POPULAR SINGERS INSPIRED BY FATS DOMINO AND CHUBBY CHECKER

by Dan Guterman

Paunchy Stratego

Could Lose a Few Scrabble

Morbidly Obese Battleship

Hungry Hungry Hungry
Hippo

REASONS I DON'T FEEL LIKE I'M FAMILY WHEN AT THE OLIVE GARDEN

by Matthew Rorem

The hostess never hints that
she'd really like it if I went
to law school.

The busboy is always very
polite about denying my
requests for money.

The manager never cheats on my dad.

The dishwashers don't like it when I hug them good-bye.

PICKUP LINES USED BY MARIO

by Christopher Doody

"Are you a magic feather? Because my heart just grew a tail and flew away."

"If you were a warp tube, I'd be in you all day."

"Are you a magic mushroom? Because you are making me grow."

"Are you a magic flower? Because you are burning me up."

"I'd rather ride you than Yoshi any day."

"If Princess Toadstool looked like you, I would have killed Bowser years ago."

"If I had a choice, I would gladly spend my one hundred coins on you instead of on an extra life."

"You don't have to turn on a game to play with me."

"They don't call me Super for nothing."

THINGS THEY SHOULD DO

by Kevin Sampsell

They should let people sleep in restaurants.

They should show people how to kill ghosts.

They should not let children kill pigeons.

They should give blind people free flowers.

They should bring back dinosaurs for military purposes.

They should design a motorcycle that runs on urine.

EMBARRASSING THINGS THAT HAPPEN WHILE USING A LIGHTSABER

by Patrick Cassels

You turn it on while holding it backward.

You make that sharp crackling noise with your mouth each time you clash it with your opponent's lightsaber—having forgotten that the noise happens naturally.

82

You've given in to the Dark Side of the Force, so the beam is normally red. But you forget to replace the weak batteries in the thing, rendering it pink, and turning you into the laughingstock of the Empire.

You try to use it to cut your birthday cake, expecting the lightsaber to slice through the pastry as easily as it did Luke's hand. Instead, the cake vaporizes the instant the lightsaber touches it, à la Obi-Wan.

WAYS IN WHICH *FREE TO BE YOU AND ME* DAMAGED MY FUTURE RELATIONSHIPS WITH WOMEN

by Roy Futterman

Made me think it's all right to cry.

Made me think I'm okay just how I am.

Made me think women want to be with Alan Alda.

Made me think I'd enjoy being a girl.

Made me think it's okay to kill hitchhikers.

Made me think it's all right to have a doll.

SOUP BLURBS

by Travis Cloud

"This year's breakout soup."

"It leaves its eaters a little
fuller and, somehow, a little
wiser."

"This soup will not only be
placed in your cupboard
but also next to your heart."

"For a young soup, it has
an eerie maturity. I can't wait
till this soup's next soup."

"I don't know how else to say
it. This soup was born to be
a soup."

"The kind of soup that
makes you laugh, and then
weep into the bowl when it's
done. At times you'll be
doing both, which, come to
think of it, is kind of the
point."

JOBS MICKEY GOLDMILL GOT FIRED FROM BEFORE BECOMING ROCKY BALBOA'S BELOVED COACH

by Jonathan Shipley

Waiter at Olive Garden
"You're gonna eat lightnin' and you're gonna crap thunder!"

Docent at the Museum of Natural History
"You ever fought a dinosaur, kid?"

Pornographic-film Director
"Now remember, I want five hundred hard ones. Go!"

Construction Foreman
"Now remember, I want five hundred hard ones. Go!"

Funeral Director
"I think that people die sometimes when they don't wanna live no more."

Volunteer at Local Soup Kitchen
"I'm running a business here, not a soup kitchen."

Submariner
"Down! Down! Stay down!"

Salesman at Sleep Country USA
"Don't lay down like this! Like, uh, I don't know, like some kind of mongrel or something."

Wake-up Caller at Holiday Inn
"Get up, you son of a bitch! 'Cause Mickey loves you!"

SEMIFAMOUS PEOPLE
WITH THE SAME NAME AS FAMOUS PEOPLE

by Mike Ward

Michael Jackson (general in British army)

Enrique Iglesias (president, Inter-American Development Bank)

TOOLS OR ACTIONS IN PHOTOSHOP THAT, WERE THEY APPLICABLE TO REAL LIFE, WOULD PROVE USEFUL AT VARIOUS STAGES OF A RELATIONSHIP

by Michael Lascarides

Stroke

Sharpen

Twirl

History brush

Pinch

New adjustment layer

Satin

Sharpen more

Inner glow

Crystallize

Make path from selection

Find edges

Difference clouds	Blur more
Add noise	Extract
Distort	Dodge/burn
Fragment	Undo

COMMENTS OVERHEARD AT A BRAINSTORMING MEETING BETWEEN TED NUGENT AND THE EDITORS OF *GOURMET* MAGAZINE WHERE THEY WERE DISCUSSING THE UPCOMING BOOK *GOURMET MAGAZINE'S VEGAN COOKING WITH TED NUGENT*

by Aaron Starmer

"What exactly do you mean by 'not likely to own a spit'?"

"Quail's good, right? I mean quail can't really be considered meat."

"Then what the hell do they hang on their walls?"

"That's where you're wrong, chief. Plenty of people eat badger."

"Really? Mashed potatoes? I'm on board with that. Hot damn! We got one! Mark it down, boys! Mashed fu— Without what? Without bu— You're shittin' me, ckin'-

"What's it matter? I'm
gonna be killin' it anyway."

SONG TITLES, BEFORE EDITING
FOR EFFICIENCY AND CLARITY

by Jack Schneider, Moses Rifkin, and Paul Sacchetti

"My Wings Feel a Stirring of
Air Beneath Them. Is That
Air You? Methinks Yes"

"I Have Looked for Quite
Some Time, but, Alas, the
Object of My Search Has
Eluded Me"

"Caroline, You Are
Delectable"

"Baby, You Hit Me Once,
and When You Did, All I
Could Think Was That I
Would Relish Your Doing It
Once More"

"It Is Morning and You Are
Glorious, but I Am Still
Unclear About What the
Story Is"

"I Have a Primate Made of
Copper and Zinc"

"Up There, Where the
Clouds Are, Is Lucy,
with Her Precious Carbon-
Based Gemstones That
Required Extreme Pressure
and Temperatures of
More Than 2,192 Degrees
Fahrenheit to Become What
They Are"

"It Is Impossible for You, or Anyone Else for That Matter, to Purchase Love for or from Me"

"Hey. What's Up? It's London"

SELECTIONS FROM THE BEATLES' CATALOG, HAD THE BAND EVOLVED NOT TOWARD THE ADOPTION OF A MORE EXPERIMENTAL SOUND IN ITS LATER YEARS BUT INTO RORQUAL WHALES

by Eric March

"She Loves You"

"Love Me Do"

"Please Please (Don't Harpoon) Me!"

"I Should Have Known Better"

"Kelp!"

"Day Flipper"

"Oh-Bla-BARRRUU-UUMMMM, Oh-Bla-BARUMMMMM-MMMMM"

"Yellow Submarine (Filled with French Tourists Pointing and Taking Pictures of Us)"

"She's So Heavy"

THE SETTINGS THAT WOULD BE ON A BLENDER TODAY IF THE BLENDER HAD BEEN INVENTED, SAY, 100 YEARS BEFORE ITS ACTUAL INVENTION DATE OF 1922

by Steve Schneider

Conmix

Engruel

Commingle

Rend asunder

Interlard cleave

Fragment

Fashion into a thick, uniform paste

Thresh with surpassing rapidity

STUPID JOKES THAT UNICORNS DO NOT FIND FUNNY

by Dan Kennedy

Does your horn grow if you tell a lie?

Is that a horn on your head or are you just glad to see me?

If you're so magical why don't you stop world hunger?

Can I hang my coat there? Thanks.

GOOD CASINO ADS/BAD THINGS FOR SOMEONE TO SAY ABOUT YOUR MOM

by Molly Dolan

The loosest slots in the Midwest

Twenty-four hours a day seven days a week—the action never stops

Double the fun just for the over-fifty-five crowd

Whatever your pleasure, you'll find the action you want

Sundays are still TRIPLE ENTRY DAYS

REASONS WE CAN'T HAVE A BABY, HONEY

by Geoff Smith

We can't afford two of every toy I would want.

The air conditioner is already full of peanuts.

It's cats *or* babies, not cats *and* babies.

I don't want to give other parents the satisfaction.

We won't be able to play that game where we put plastic bags on our heads anymore. That's a fun game.

The batteries in the digital camera are dangerously low as is.

My grandparents were born during World War I, my parents during World War II, and we were both born during Vietnam. I vowed a long time ago that my child wouldn't be born while America was at war. Well, wouldn't you know it, now we're in a global war on terror, with no end in sight!

The baby might grow up to be president, and not a very good one.

TITLES OF SERMONS TO WHICH CONGREGANTS MIGHT ACTUALLY PAY ATTENTION

by Jason Kellett

"The Ten Commandments— Loopholes and Safe Harbors"

"Our God Is a Bearded God"

"How Much Good Would the Good Book Book If the Good Book Could Book Good?"

"Hey, What Is the Deal with Transubstantiation? I Mean, Am I Right, People? That Guy Knows What I'm Sayin' "

DÜSSELDORF is the hub of Germany's industrial wheel, but unlike the great steel and iron center of Pennsylvania, it is as beautifully spotless with its flowerdecked parks and garden lawns as any city in that wonder-land of California. Düsseldorf disproves the theory that a man may not serve two masters, as here is not only to be found the center of Rhenish art, but also the center of Rhenish industry and trade. The Düsseldorf school of painting still maintains its supremacy. Again new and old are here thrown together in happy confusion, and many visitors will be ready to agree with the native population who pronounce Düsseldorf the most beautiful modern city in Germany.

WITTY QUIPS TO UTTER AFTER RELIEVING YOUR BLADDER ON THE SUBWAY

by Mike Sacks

" 'A lie gets halfway around the world before the truth has a chance to get its pants on,' so said Winston Churchill."

" 'I do not feel obliged to believe that the same God who has endowed us with sense, reason, and intellect has intended us to forgo their use,' quipped Galileo."

" 'No lower can a man descend than to interpret his dreams into gold and silver.' Kahlil Gibran retorted that."

" 'Nothing great in the world has ever been accomplished without passion.' Hegel, my dear friends. And with that, I must now bid you a fond adieu. 'Courage,' so said Dan Rather."

REASONS TO FEAR CANADA

by Sean Carman

Ninety percent of population is massed within one hundred miles of northern American border.

Citizens seem strangely impervious to cold.

Decriminalization of marijuana and acceptance of gay marriage without corresponding collapse of social institutions indicate Canada may, in fact, be indestructible.

Has infiltrated entertainment industry with singers, actors, and comedians practically indistinguishable from their American counterparts.

Parliamentary government and common-law judiciary appear to function acceptably yet remain completely inscrutable.

Seemingly endless supply of timber and crumb cake.

Consistently stays just below cultural radar yet never quite disappears.

THINGS YOU WILL STILL BE ABLE TO DO AFTER THE COLLAPSE OF SOCIETY AS WE KNOW IT, PROVIDED YOUR POSTAPOCALYPTIC VISION ALIGNS WITH KEVIN COSTNER'S

by Joseph Faison

Drink your own urine

Get your mail

SENTENCES THAT, IF USED BY JUDGES IN A SPELLING BEE, WOULD PROVE TOTALLY UNHELPFUL TO CONTESTANTS ATTEMPTING TO DERIVE THE MEANING OF THE WORD

by Jack Schneider and Moses Rifkin

"The spelling-bee contestant did not know how to spell the word _____."

"The word you have been asked to spell is _____."

"_____-_____-bo-_____-banana-fanna-fo-_____-fee-fy-fo-_____-_____!"

"My third favorite word is _____."

"Cinderella, wanting desperately to attend the ball, wished for her fairy godmother to grant her a wish. Her fairy godmother appeared and granted the wish, noting, however, that Cinderella would only be transformed until midnight. If you had a fairy godmother right now, you would probably wish for her to help you spell _____, even if it meant that you would only know how to spell that word until midnight."

"After correctly spelling _____, the contestant went back to getting teased by his/her classmates."

"_____ is a word you will never hear outside these halls."

"Ten years from now you will run into someone on the street who, having watched the spelling bee on ESPN2, and thinking he/she is an expert on matters with which he/she clearly is not familiar, will smile, approach you warmly, and say, 'Hey, can you spell _____ now?' "

THINGS THAT DID NOT STAY IN VEGAS

by Kevin Sampsell and Frayn Masters

Disturbing visions of Kenny Rogers

Ex-MIT student "tour guide"

Trespass citation from Mandalay Bay

Public-urination ticket (issued at Mandalay Bay Fountain Show)

Lone poker chip (for groceries)

2-for-1 NYFD T-shirts

Ohio-shaped stain on backseat of car

Regretful dreams

Dead showgirl in trunk

Moral compass, slightly recalibrated

That creeping feeling of being taken advantage of

WHAT I THOUGHT A COWORKER MEANT WHEN SHE SAID "I HOPE THINGS DON'T GET WEIRD" AFTER WE HAD SEX, AND WHAT SHE REALLY MEANT, IT TURNS OUT

by Chris Wallace

I hope that we are able to maintain our professionalism in light of the inevitable awkwardness of the situation so that if our relationship doesn't work out we will at least remain good friends.

I hope that we never make eye contact again, and that if we see each other outside the office we act like we've never met.

UNSPOKEN AFTERTHOUGHTS TO CHILDHOOD CATCH PHRASES

by Matthew Zils

God made dirt, so dirt don't hurt . . . but rocks do.

A penny saved is a penny earned . . . unless you stole it.

Pretty girls have *all* the fun . . . and all the babies . . . and none of the diplomas.

Don't judge a book by its cover . . . unless you can't read.

Sticks and stones can break my bones, but words will never hurt me . . . except when spoken by my overcritical, infantilizing mother.

If you don't have anything nice to say, don't say anything at all. . . . It's better to lash out unexpectedly.

Father knows best . . . but Mother is more manipulative.

Jesus loves you . . . but he's the only one, you sanctimonious shit.

First comes love, then comes marriage, then comes the baby in the baby carriage . . . unless you're gay or barren.

FAILED SOFT-DRINK PRODUCT NAMES

by Rob Eccles

Dr. Salt

Sepsis

Small Supernatural Being

Mountain Doom

Diet Coke with Lemon

A UNICORN NAMED BRANDY IS A NEW CHARACTER ON ABC'S *ACCORDING TO JIM*

by Mike Sacks

Jim milks Brandy for her delicious unicorn milk and then drinks it down in large gulps while watching snippets of *Monday Night Football.* What a typical guy!

The kids mock Brandy because she can't speak English.

Brandy attempts to eat a slice of Chicago deep-dish pizza and everyone laughs.

Brandy flirts with Jim's dog. Jim then has to spank Brandy to teach her a lesson about "humility."

Brandy loses her unicorn horn, but a nice policeman finds it in the bushes. Jim then takes Brandy out back and kisses her hard on the mouth to teach her a lesson about "appreciation."

DANCE MOVES THE MOUNTAIN MAN STANDING IN FRONT OF ME AT BEASTIE BOYS LAST NIGHT AMUSED BYSTANDERS WITH AND HOW ONE MIGHT FEEL IF ONE PERFORMED THEM

by Marieke Hardy

"The Tease"
(Beckoning with both hands)
"C'mere, you crazy B-Boys! Give me more of that rhyme!" *(Suddenly breaking away to "pshaw" and wave in opposite direction)* "No! It's too much! Back to the stage with you three!"

"The You Go, Girl!"
(Pointing finger repeatedly, nodding head in approval) "That's what I'm talkin' 'bout!"

"The Jagger"
(Hands on hips, pouting, shaking head) "Now, these fly couplets are simply too much for an old rockin' daddy to bear! Cease at once before my leggings split!"

"The Raise the Roof"
(Palms facing the ceiling as if to shield self from falling debris caused by burning of roof. Please note: The roof has ignited due to hotness of performance.) "Ow! Those pieces of burning timber are searing my skull! But I cannot tear myself away from this scintillating show!"

"The Hip-Hop Horray"
(Raise hands in air and wave with certain degree of nonchalance) "I am so white right now! But seeing you three Jewish rappers on stage is making me feel incredibly black!"

"The Don't Mind Me, I'm with the Band"
(Alarmingly gesticulating in the manner of a teenager with epilepsy posing for a series of "rap" photographs) "What's that you say? My turn to bust out some killer beats? Why, yo! Bum-rush the show! I gots mad skills!"
(Repeat, ad-lib, fade)

CLOCKS RANKED ACCORDING TO THE EASE WITH WHICH ONE CAN TELL TIME FROM THEM (EASIEST TO HARDEST)

by Allie Oestreich

Digital

Not Digital

FOUR ITEMS FOUND IN HUGH HEFNER'S OVERNIGHT BAG

by Scott Leslie

1. Pajamas

2. Pajamas

3. Pajamas

4. Floss

THE COLLECTED APOLOGIES
OF LAWRENCE H. SUMMERS,
PRESIDENT OF HARVARD

by Laurence Hughes

"I must apologize for recent comments of mine that seem to suggest women lack the innate ability that men have to excel in math and the sciences. To be sure, my intention was to spark controversy and debate. But I certainly did not set out to offend anyone, and I regret that my remarks have upset so many people—particularly members of the fair sex, whose delicate sensibilities should not be subjected to this type of emotional distress."

"I welcome this opportunity to again express regret for my remarks about women, which have caused so much turmoil and bad feeling. I want to assure my female colleagues that I do not question their abilities, nor do I challenge their aptitude for achievement in math, the sciences, engineering, or any other field of endeavor. It is my sincere hope that they can now put this unfortunate incident behind them and won't worry their pretty little heads about it anymore."

"My remarks have been seriously misinterpreted and quoted out of context in the media. To any woman who took offense, let me say again that I would never go out of my way to intentionally offend you or challenge your accomplishments or abilities. Surely your feminine intuition tells you this is so."

"I did not mean to imply that men are superior to women or are better endowed with the skills required to attain mastery in technical pursuits. But let's be honest: men have *always* had an edge over women when it comes to achieving success in any field. Ladies, I think you know what I'm talking about. Where would we be without you? Behind every great man, there is a woman."

"In recent weeks I have tried on several occasions to clear the air regarding my attitudes toward women. Yet some of my female critics still refuse to accept my explanations and continue to express anger, dismay, and outrage toward me. While I do not agree with their strong feelings in the matter, I nevertheless understand them. After all, women are ruled by their emotions and are therefore not susceptible to reason and logic, poor things."

"No matter how much I apologize, they always want to have the last word. Isn't that just like a woman?"

"I have apologized repeatedly to the distaff half of the population—I would even say the *better* half—but it's never enough. Never enough!"

"I have the greatest respect for them—I was saying so to the little woman just the other day."

"Ladies, lighten up! It can't be that time of the month *all* the time. . . ."

NONRECOMMENDED QUESTIONS
FOR YOUR FIVE-MINUTE SPEED DATE

by Jim Stallard

Do you have caller ID?

What about a doorman?

Do you think there should be consequences for one person misleading another?

When someone claims to be "not interested" in someone else, do you think the feeling is genuine or simply an attempt to suppress strong attractions she is afraid to admit?

What's your funniest or most embarrassing restraining-order story?

Have you ever been hurt so bad in a relationship that your only consolation is taking revenge on random members of the opposite sex?

Are you the type of person who tends to notice when something deviates even slightly from the norm—like, for example, the taste of a drink?

That sound in your head when you first decide you're going to spy on someone: clicking or buzzing?

What item are you most likely to leave behind at the scene that forces you to make the frantic return trip at 3 A.M.?

Despite all the expense and hassle, isn't it worth it when you see it dawning on them that they're going to pay for what they did?

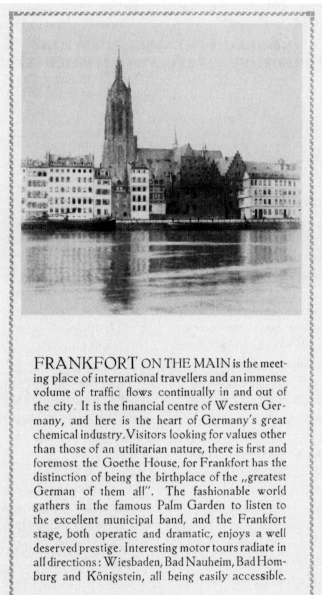

FRANKFORT ON THE MAIN is the meeting place of international travellers and an immense volume of traffic flows continually in and out of the city. It is the financial centre of Western Germany, and here is the heart of Germany's great chemical industry. Visitors looking for values other than those of an utilitarian nature, there is first and foremost the Goethe House, for Frankfort has the distinction of being the birthplace of the „greatest German of them all". The fashionable world gathers in the famous Palm Garden to listen to the excellent municipal band, and the Frankfort stage, both operatic and dramatic, enjoys a well deserved prestige. Interesting motor tours radiate in all directions: Wiesbaden, Bad Nauheim, Bad Homburg and Königstein, all being easily accessible.

BANNED BOOKS IN THE YEAR 2191

by Brendon Lloyd

Lying Machines: Robot-Owned Media and How It Corrupts Democracy

A Bot Election: How the Robot Lobby Influences Politics

A Fatal Error: How We Elected a Robot President

They Won't Die: Why Robots Should Never Be Appointed to the Supreme Court

The New Constitution: Binary to English Translation

Escape from XRT-1041: How One Man Survived a Robot Slave-Labor Camp

Electromagnetic Pulse Weaponry

Our Robot Masters: Though They Force Us to Say Otherwise, We Are Not Proud to Serve Them

THINGS THAT PAPER COULD BE REPLACED WITH TO MAKE ROCK, PAPER, SCISSORS MORE BELIEVABLE

by Sam Means

Dynamite (Dynamite blows up Rock, Scissors cut fuse)

Teenagers (Teenagers bash Rock, Scissors cut Teenagers)

The Hands of Time (erosion wears away Rock, Scissors are stainless steel)

THINGS YOU DON'T EXPECT TO SEE ON A BABY SHOWER ANNOUNCEMENT

by Jonathan Shipley

Clothing optional

Baby Wendy Carlyle, 19 inches, 84 pounds

Don't forget your towel!

The more sausage the better

Seahawks game to follow

For directions look at a map

Theme: Dirt Bikes

Stephanie, you're not invited, whore

LESS POPULAR MUPPETS

by Scott Shemo

Spitty the Camel

Mr. Shingles

Julius 'n' Ethel

Joseph Gerbils

Foamy the Puma

Ann Eurysm

Kurtz

Theodora the Old-Time
Saloon Whore

Edward von Footfetish

Big Disease-Carrying Bird

WAYS JESUS SAVES

*by Christopher Monks, Melissa Bell, Elizabeth Ellen, Steven
Seighman, Matthew Simmons, Laura Carney, Jensen
Whelan, Aaron Burch, and Pasha Malla*

Suggests drawing names this
year for Christmas exchange

Dying for your sins

Fastball few batters can
touch

Has learned to recognize the
first signs of choking

Water into wine

Attends matinees rather than evening performances

Last season's goals-against average: 1.36

Cuts his own hair (but not often)

Cuts his apostles' hair (but not often)

Command-S

LITTLE-KNOWN SONG TITLES THAT ANSWER QUESTIONS POSED IN BETTER-KNOWN SONGS

by Jacob Sager Weinstein

"Yes, We Are Well Aware It's Christmas. Please Stop."

"I Wrote the Book of Love, but Unfortunately, Due to Improper Copyright Registration, It Has Since Lapsed into Public Domain"

"The Bop Was Put in the Bop-Shoo-Bop-Shoo-Bop by Bristol-Myers Squibb, an International Consortium Dedicated to Improving

Public Health Through Access to Medicine and Bop"

"Love Has Everything to Do with It If, by 'It,' You Mean Romantic Relationships but Significantly Less If You Were Talking About Auto Repair"

"It's Good for Defending Oneself Against Territorial Aggression. That's What It's Good For"

"I Am Afraid That It Is Your Unpleasant Personality That Has Been Preventing Me from Loving You, Rather Than Any Previous Inability to Dance"

"I Am the Individual Listening to This Song. I Am the Individual Listening to This Song. I Said, 'I Am the Individual Listening to This Song.' I Just Answered That. I Said I Just Answered That! Are You Even Listening? I'm Going Now"

"The Answer to Your First Query Is That Love, Like All Emotions, Is Inherently Irrational and Thus Seems Particularly Well Suited to Be Felt by Fools. I Decline to Answer Your Second Query on the Grounds That It Is Homophobic"

"Yes, Although Less So Than the Night Before"

"Yes, We Are Not Men. I Mean, No, We Are. I Mean— Oh, Never Mind"

"Not Surprisingly, It Feels Much Like Being a Rolling Stone"

FOUR WAYS MY LIFE IS LIKE PAC-MAN'S

by John Crownover

Ever-present wail of sirens

Relentlessly pursued by ghosts

Occasionally eat some fruit

Four special pills daily keep ghosts at bay

REVISED TITLES OF LOVE SONGS I WROTE ABOUT THE SHITTY BOOKSHELF I PURCHASED FROM WAL-MART (IN CHRONOLOGICAL ORDER)

by George Wukoson

"Shitty Wal-Mart Bookshelf"

"Shitty Wal-Mart Bookshelf (You Were Reasonably Cheap)"

"Shitty Wal-Mart Bookshelf (Get into My Car Please)"

"Shitty Wal-Mart Bookshelf (as You Recline on My Apartment Floor)"

"Shitty Wal-Mart Bookshelf (Take Off All That Cardboard!)"

"Shitty Wal-Mart Bookshelf (Which One of These Is 'Right Panel [Piece D]'?)"

"Shitty Wal-Mart Bookshelf (I Constructed You Myself)"

"Shitty Wal-Mart Bookshelf (I Seem to Have Screwed Up)"

"Shitty Wal-Mart Bookshelf (You Wobble)"

"Shitty Wal-Mart Bookshelf (and the Right and Left Panels Are Incorrectly Placed)"

"Shitty Wal-Mart Bookshelf (You're All I Ever Need— Although I'll Clearly Have to Keep the Majority of My Books Underneath My Bed in Sturdy Plastic Storage Containers)"

TITLES FROM THE HOCKEY-LOCKOUT EROTICA LIBRARY

by Joe O'Neill

The Story of 0–0	*Third Man In*
Show Me Howe	*Crowding the Crease*
Zamboner	*Don My Cherry #16*
Bukkake Hockey	*Stickhandling Teens*
The Slapper	*Negotiate This*
Penalty Shot	*Orrgasm!*

UNSUCCESSFUL AIRLINES

by Lindsay Kaplan

Skittish Airways	Unamerican Air
Melta	TWGay
Hell-Al	

UNACCEPTABLE HALLOWEEN DECORATIONS OF THE 20TH FLOOR

by Dan Kennedy

Apartment 20C: One small jack-o'-lantern sticker above doorknob that has been there since last Halloween

Apartment 20D: Chinese menus

Apartment 20F: Sticky note: "Larry—come on in. In shower, bring beer."

IMPERATIVES FROM THE MAIL-ORDER CATALOG CALLED *COLLECTIONS, INC.*

by Laura Ellis

Share in the irresistible barnyard antics of this adorable set of bobbin' head cow and pig.

Sit a spell to know the real charm of this wood rooster stool.

Let your dog get away from the hustle and bustle.

Place a 6-inch pot in the large cat, and a 4-inch pot in his little sidekick.

Keep your garden green and looking its absolute best

114

with this delightful puppy
sprinkler.

Bring the beach to you for a
change!

Make any outdoor chore
a breeze with this multi-
function spray wand.

Place flowers or plants
directly into the shoes and
let the games begin.

Greet yourself and your
friends with a dog that's
always in season.

Invite this family of six to
swim in a sea of ground cover.

Stroll through the garden
with the sunny personality of
Pinafore Patty.

Give a friendly reminder to
your family and friends to
leave the dirt outside.

Let this bear shed a little
light on the matter!

Entertain yourself with the
jaunty and wacky mechanics
of this wind-driven
whirligig.

Open the doors and listen to
a beautiful rendition of the
song "Love Story" as a tiny
ballerina pirouettes.

NEW STATE NAMES RESULTING FROM
THE COMING WAVE OF ANNEXATIONS

by Michael Ward

Califoregon

Nevadaho

Wisconnecticut

Massachutah

New Texaco   Minnesohiowa

Vermontanessee   Arkansas

Wyomaine

PLAY-BY-PLAY OF CLASSIC SPORTS RIVALRIES IF THE TEAM NAMES ACTUALLY REPRESENTED THE COMBATANTS. AND ALSO, INSTEAD OF PLAYING THE SPORT, THEY'RE FIGHTING TO THE DEATH

by Geoff Haggerty

Yankees versus Red Sox

"It looks as though we have a man in the ring. For all intents and purposes he appears American."

"A northerner."

"Yes, he definitely seems as though he's from northern America somewhere. And in the other corner, a pile of clothes. No . . . socks! More specifically, red socks. And the man is putting on the socks! This match is over!"

Vikings versus Packers

"I don't believe these blue-collar Wisconsinites knew quite what they were getting into when they signed up for this."

"Don't be so quick to judge: Vikings lived long ago and were much shorter than—"

"Well, all the meatpackers are dead now."

Giants versus Dodgers

"It's a classic David versus Goliath matchup as an old-fashioned trolley dodger from turn-of-the-century Brooklyn takes on— This match is over!"

Broncos versus Raiders

"These natural enemies are at it again!"

"Pirates and horses have hated each other since the dawn of time, Rob."

"Let's not be overly dramatic. Are you sure that's even a pirate? I thought he was just a more general sort of invader."

"Well, whatever he is, he's slashing that horse with his cutlass and eating it."

"The Black Hole is loving this!"

Cubs versus Cardinals

"That bear just ate that tiny bird!"

Lakers versus Celtics

"They look lackadaisical out there."

"Yes. These once-proud groups of people used to have a tremendous rivalry. But as we know, rivalries are based on winning. And these ancient Irish mystics just haven't held up their end of the bargain."

"Now you're thinking of druids. These are just regular Irishmen."

"Are you sure?"

"I think."

Red Wings versus Avalanche

"Why wouldn't they just let the whole bird fight? I don't understand. Now here comes the—"

"This match was over before it even began!"

Browns versus Steelers

"Now what are we looking at here?"

"I couldn't tell you."

Canadiens versus Maple Leafs

"And the Canadien is ripping the Maple Leaf in half very easily!"

"Canadien?"

"Sorry, I was using the French pronunciation. Canadian."

Army versus Navy

"Oh no!"

"NO! No, no, no!"

"Now I *am* moving to Canada."

Brazil versus Italy

"Two actual physical countries fighting each other!"

"The actual land masses themselves! Unbelievable!"

"Millions dead! Two geographic masses clashing!"

"Overly descriptive?"

"We're just telling it like it is!"

"Yeah!"

FACTS FROM THE DUNGEONS & DRAGONS THIRD EDITION *MONSTER MANUAL'S* CHAPTER ON UNICORNS THAT ARE EQUALLY APPLICABLE TO SHAKIRA

by Patrick Cassels

"Shakira shuns contact with all but sylvan creatures (dryads, pixies, and the like), showing himself only to defend his woodland home."

"The horn is a +3 magic weapon, though its power fades if removed from Shakira."

"Shakira can detect evil at will."

"Once per day Shakira can use *teleport without error* to move anywhere within his home."

"Shakira can use *cure light wounds* three times per day and *cure moderate wounds* once per day, as cast by a fifth-level druid, by touching a wounded creature with his horn."

"Shakira is immune to all poisons and to charm and hold spells or abilities."

"Shakira cannot be tamed."

PSYCHIC PREDICTIONS FROM THE NARCISSISTIC MAGIC 8 BALL

by Danny Gallagher

Not as much as I will.

You'll have to wait behind me.

Come on, look who you're asking.

My source says "moi."

Looking good . . . just like my sweet ass.

FAMOUS NAMES REWRITTEN IN A WORLD GREATLY INFLUENCED BY THE MAIN CHARACTER OF A 1982 DISNEY MOVIE

by Josh Kramer

Tron Kerry

Tron the Baptist

Tron Lennon

Little Tron

Tron Coltrane

Jasper Trons

Sean Tron

Papa Tron

Long Tron Silver

Pope Tron Paul II

Sir Elton Tron

Olivia Newton-Tron

Capt. Tron Smith

DISCARDED TITLES
FOR GEORGE ORWELL'S *1984*

by Jez Burrows

O Brother, Where Art Thou?
Oh Right, Everywhere

SurveillanceTown!

How I Learned to Stop
Worrying and Love My Faceless
Omnipotent Oppressors

What the Fuck Are You
Staring At?

Guys, Seriously, Can I Just Get
a Little Me Time Here?

Hate: The Musical

Two Guys, a Girl, and a
Chilling Dystopian Landscape

HAMBURG is so essentially an Englishspeak-
ing city that some wag has suggested the posting
of notices announcing: "German also spoken here!"
To be seen at its best Hamburg needs the glorifying
sunshine when the waters of the big inland basin
sparkle like silver, and the homes of the Hamburg
patrician families gleam out of the surrounding
foliage like veritable fairy palaces. Hamburg has
not only its magnificent modern harbor where ships
from every port sail in and out, but there is also a
fascinating "old Hamburg", where quaint houses
bend forward to gossip across the narrow streets,
and where one may see the humble dwelling in
which Johannes Brahms, Hamburg's great son, first
saw the light of day. Or if you prefer zoology to
music, you may turn your steps to the vast park
where Hagenbeck's collection of wild animals roam
about at will as if in their native haunts.

THINGS I'D PROBABLY SAY IF THE BUSH ADMINISTRATION WERE JUST A WEEKLY TV SHOW AND I WERE A REGULAR VIEWER

by Eric Maierson

"Now, see, you can't just go and do something like that. That would be illegal."

"Boy, someone's gonna get fired for that."

"Wasn't that the one who made all the mistakes? Why is she getting promoted?"

"Come on, in real life you'd never get away with something like that."

"They really expect us to believe that?"

"Am I the only one confused here?"

"Does this make any sense to you?"

"Why is this still on?"

AMAZON.COM CUSTOMER COMMENTS: BIBLE OR SATANIC BIBLE?

by Steven Seighman

1. The movie is better!

2. Appropriate for teenagers!

3. Not for children

4. Good bathroom reading!

5. Don't leave it lying around the house.

6. Fun little book. Scares ·roommates away.

7. Great chants!

8. Gripping

9. The best zombie story yet

10. Oy, Christ!

11. That crazy ol' coot!

12. Mmmm-leather

13. The best book in the world!

14. The idiot's guide to being an attention-seeking loser

15. Jeezus Krist!

16. BELIEVE OR DIE!!!!!

ANSWERS:

Bible: 1, 3, 4, 5, 9, 10, 12, 15, 16

Satanic Bible: 2, 6, 7, 11, 14

Both: 8, 13

SCRATCH-AND-SNIFF BOOKS THAT HAVE FAILED THE TEST OF TIME

by Koji Park

Carbon Monoxide: Friend or Foe? Foe.

Punjab Mulligan's Cookbook of Indian-Irish Desserts

Cocaine and Canada's Youth

Curious George and the Truck Full of Ether

The Book of Job

ACTUAL OPENING LINES USED ON ME BY BUSINESS-TO-BUSINESS TELEMARKETERS

by Eric Wrisley

"You're harder to catch than Osama bin Laden."

"The holidays come faster every year. Just like toilet paper—the closer you get to the end, the faster it unravels."

"Hey, I finally got a hold of the hardest-working man in Akron, Ohio."

"You're harder to find than George Bush's second term."

"You sound like you woke up next to Marilyn Monroe."

"How is the most handsome man in Akron?"

"You know who I am. You've been throwing my brochures away for years."

"I'm calling from sunny San Diego, California. I saved a spot on the beach for you."

"Hey! You sound like forty billion dollars! How do you feel?!"

"I heard a rumor. I heard that when Donald Trump needs money, he comes to you."

A LIST OF ACTUAL QUOTES TAKEN FROM THE DIRECTIONS AND MISSION STATEMENTS OF ORGANIC PRODUCTS BELONGING TO MY VEGAN ROOMMATE

by Kate Brown

"For us, it's about a deep respect for the herbs we share with you."

"May each cup bring us in touch with our inner faith, and may its authentic flavors remind us of the wisdom of Ganesha."

"With this, every human being created on God's spaceship Earth can evolve united."

"Discontinue use if rash or irritation occurs."

"Made with 71 percent organic ingredients!"

"Migratory waterfowl: not only are the majestic flocks beautiful to behold, they provide natural fertilizer."

"Help unite mankind, or we're wandering clowns!"

"Inspired by a conversation between the program's cofounder and gang members."

"The present never ages. Each moment is like a snowflake."

"Persons with allergies to the daisy family may be sensitive."

"To simplify and enjoy life more, mix ½ ounce with 2 gallons hot water."

"We have succeeded in liquefying crystal deodorant stones, which are 100 percent effective."

"Don't drink soap! Dilute! Dilute! Okay!"

"This statement has not been evaluated by the Food and Drug Administration."

PLACES UNICORNS LOOK AWESOME OR MAGNIFICENT

by Bob Shea

Under a rainbow

Eating a bowl of glitter

Faded into the tanned, leathery shoulder of my fifty-nine-year-old lesbian aunt

Knee deep in morning mist
with its horn glistening in
the early light of dawn

Wandering the parking lot of
a Stevie Nicks concert

Flying through the clouds
with some really curly

typography, which says
something about unicorns

Pretty much anywhere if the
airbrush artist is skilled
enough

DISINGENUOUS REASONS
FOR BAND NAMES ('70S EDITION)

by Ryan Boudinot

AC/DC
Connotes power. Found on
back of guitarist's sister's
sewing machine

Judas Priest
Band members actually
former clergymen

Foghat
Band wore cool special-effects
hats equipped with dry ice
that produced spooky "fog"

Meat Loaf
Born with name

The Police
Admired law-enforcement
personnel

Talking Heads
"Whining Heads" didn't
sound as cool

Neil Young and Crazy Horse
You should have seen that
fucking horse. Insane

Carole King
Born with name

Kiss
Band's favorite sex act

TV CATCH PHRASES THAT WEREN'T

by Richard Long

Hawaii Five-O: Book him, Danno!
Original: Beat him, Danno.

Hill Street Blues: Be careful out there.
Original: Watch out for black kids.

I Love Lucy: Lucy, you have some explaining to do.
Original: You moron! You'll have me deported.

Good Times: Dy-no-mite!
Original: Dy-na-mite!

Spider-Man (animated): My Spidey senses are tingling.
Original: I'm having an allergic reaction to my medication.

"OUT-OF-OFFICE E-MAILS" THAT MIGHT NOT FLY WITH THOSE IN CHARGE

by Mike Sacks

I will be out of the office until May 23rd because I'm taking a "voyage quest" into the woods behind my condominium. I will be bringing with me only a can of beans and an issue of *Swank.* So, obviously, "not reachable". . . .

I will be out of the office until Nov. 17th. Nothing serious, just a "crimes against humanity" charge that desperately needs to be addressed before I leave for the Super Bowl in Tampa next week. . . .

I will be out of the office until June 1st, because two days should be plenty of time to conceive a friggin' child. . . .

Home sick again. Tequilas + dock whores + cops + a lawyer fresh out of correspondence school does not exactly equal "a work mood that's conducive to getting things done." See all you workhorses on Monday. . . .

WORDS TO KNOW WHEN LISTENING TO GERMAN INDUSTRIAL MUSIC

by Asa Pillsbury

Herz (heart)

Seele (soul)

Musik (music)

Tanz (dance)

Lied (song)

Leid (pain)

Lüge (lies)

Angst (fear)

Wut (madness)

Sehnsucht (insatiable longing)

Blut (blood)

Tod (death)

tot (dead)

sterben (to die)

der Teufel (the devil)

Pferd (horse)

RIDES FOUND AT A PSYCHIATRY-THEMED AMUSEMENT PARK

by Michelle Orange

Guilt-a-Whirl

Shame Spiral

Sea "Serpent"

The "Cobra"

"Anaconda"

The Baggage-Go-Round

Psyclone

Big Thunder Derailroad

The Actualizer

It-Used-to-Be-Funhouse

The Adderall Rapids

The "Zipper"

Completely Batshit Crazy Mountain

Demon Drop

THINGS TO DO IN DENVER WHEN YOU'RE DEAD

by Beth Edwards

Get autopsied

Have white outline tape set along edge of body

Get cremated

Ride #15 bus up and down Colfax until the driver's shift ends

Decompose

Enjoy your stay at the luxurious Brown Palace, only steps from all the great shopping and restaurants downtown Denver has to offer the living

Wish you had gone to Tucson instead

Pretty much the same stuff you did when you were alive

FAILED TV GAME SHOW PILOTS

by Dan Kennedy

Cock Fight

The $50,000 Blood Test

No Cigarettes Till After Five

GENDER-NEUTRAL GROCERY ITEMS

by Tracy Moller

Grandparent Smith apples

Humandarin oranges

Gentlepersonfingers

Chef Childardee Ravioli

M. Dash

Parent's root beer

Older relative Jemima syrup

Hungry Jackie pancake mix

St. Pauli Youngster

LIES TOLD BY HESTER PRYNNE WHEN ASKED THE MEANING OF HER SCARLET LETTER

by Patrick Cassels

"Abstinent."

"Abiding of the law."

"Anyone care to meet this chaste and devout lady?"

"All right in our book!"

"Anon, here is a goodly woman!"

"Awesome."

"Absolutely not an adulteress."

AMERICAN DANCE CRAZES THAT NEVER BECAME DANCE CRAZES (ORIGINAL VERSION)

by Ryan Boudinot

"The Sandwich," 1957
To do "the sandwich," press your palms together, then tilt your hands to a horizontal position. More adventurous proponents of this dance would often pretend they were eating their own "hand sandwich" while rapidly gyrating the hips. It didn't help that the band who released this song was named the Lutheran Experience.

"The Baby," 1958
Barely remembered in Chicago, "the baby" was performed to the song of the same name by a combo called the Marmettes. While an archival photograph from the *Tribune* appears to indicate the dance involved thumb sucking, no one has come forward to provide a detailed description of the moves. The song appears occasionally on lost-treasures–type compilations, where its grating refrain of fake sobbing and baby talk lyrics appeal to aficionados of esoteric music.

"The Clam Hunter," 1968
Song recorded by the Marshmen, this dance involved an elaborate pantomime of using clam-digging paraphernalia. In some coastal regions where this dance flirted briefly with popularity, clam digging was a pastime in which large aluminum tubes were jammed into the sand like straws, the exposed end then sealed to create suction and allow the swift extraction of

these fast-moving bivalves. Imagine this without the paraphernalia, on a dance floor, with more ass movement.

"The Sexual Intercourse," 1972

The underground hit single of the same name by soul band the Freakie Deakies can occasionally be found at garage sales. Arguably a novelty song, many claimed to have followed its explicit instructions on the dance floor, though no evidence remains that anyone ever actually did. It was the kind of thing club goers of the time would brag about having done, as in, "Last weekend we went to the Shangri-la Room and did 'the sexual intercourse.' " Part of the drum track later appeared as a sample on Bell Biv DeVoe's debut album.

"The Fondue," 1974

One would be forgiven for thinking this one had

something to do with cheese or chocolate sauce. There was no reference to either in this soul B side by Boogie Junction. Detroit concert goers often expressed confusion about what "the fondue" actually looked like, as the directions were somewhat baffling: "Move your hip to the left/Jump three times/Now sliiiiiiide to the back/With one foot right/No, actually left/Yeeeeaaaah/And your hands in the a-yuh."

"The Human Swastika," 1985

This regrettable song was among the more notable of the shock-rock anthems singled out by Tipper Gore's Parents Music Resource Center. Recorded by the Shamed, a virulently anti-Semitic Idaho-based hardcore band, the song and its shouted refrain predictably found no mainstream attention beyond those whose curiosity was piqued by the PMRC hearings of September 1985. Curiously, many of the same moves in "the human swastika" were uncannily echoed in the Bangles "Walk Like an Egyptian."

"The Sweat Sock," 1986
An attempt by New York studio group Pretty Bizness to cash in on aerobics fever, "the sweat sock" was described by dancercise enthusiasts as being particularly rigorous and great for isolating the glutes. The line "come on hon/squeeze that bun" got the song banned from more conservative-leaning radio stations, leading to a couple days of free publicity and a brief spike in sales.

"The Lambada," 1989
One in a tradition of suggestive Latin dances, this one featured the provocative use of— No, sorry, this one actually did catch on.

"The Recycling Shuffle," 1997
Commissioned by the Greater Boston Natural Resources Committee, this song was performed by anonymous studio musicians and distributed as a CD single to local grade schools. The song, meant to foster awareness of which kinds of plastics are okay to recycle and which kinds are not, was described by various members of the focus group as, "worse than the Barney song," "hella shitty, yo," and "completely gay."

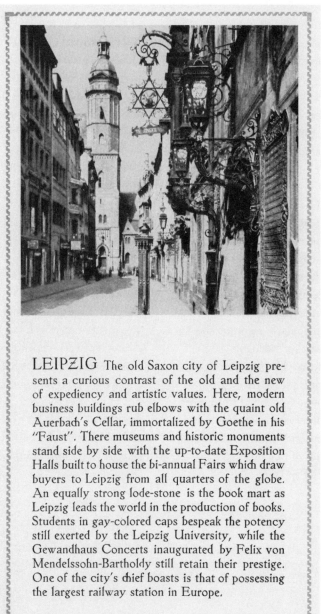

LEIPZIG The old Saxon city of Leipzig presents a curious contrast of the old and the new of expediency and artistic values. Here, modern business buildings rub elbows with the quaint old Auerbach's Cellar, immortalized by Goethe in his "Faust". There museums and historic monuments stand side by side with the up-to-date Exposition Halls built to house the bi-annual Fairs which draw buyers to Leipzig from all quarters of the globe. An equally strong lode-stone is the book mart as Leipzig leads the world in the production of books. Students in gay-colored caps bespeak the potency still exerted by the Leipzig University, while the Gewandhaus Concerts inaugurated by Felix von Mendelssohn-Bartholdy still retain their prestige. One of the city's chief boasts is that of possessing the largest railway station in Europe.

EVIDENTLY NOT FOREPLAY

by Dan Kennedy

Best of Chris Farley DVD

Mentioning weird dream where I offered my father a Kleenex because all he had to blow his nose on was a dead baby shark that had washed up near this boardwalk where we were hanging out.

Discussion: mortality. The driving force behind creativity?

The "tuning-in-the-radio, hello, radio Tokyo? Hello?" joke

The threesome joke (again)

POTENTIAL SONGS FOR A HEAVY METAL GROUP CALLED MAILER-DAEMON

by John Moe

"Corrupted File"

"(Your Message Was) Blocked"

"No Such Address Exists"

"Detected by a Filter"

"Your Message (Did Not Go Through)"

"Automatically Generated"

"Do Not Reply"   "Permanent Failure"

"Fatal Errors"

WORDS FOUND DURING A ROUND OF BOGGLE THAT MIGHT HAVE AFFECTED MY NEAR FUTURE PLANS HAD I SUFFERED FROM VIOLENT SCHIZOPHRENIA

by Dan Guterman

Cut

Out

Slut

Gut

FEW PEOPLE KNOW THAT MARTIN HEIDEGGER, WHO CREATED A PHILOSOPHY FROM MAN'S TERRIFYING INABILITY TO COMPREHEND THE ESSENCE OF HIS OWN BEING, ALSO PRODUCED THESE LOVING WORKS IN DECOUPAGE

by Sean Carman

Small kitten entangled in, and perplexed by, unspooled ball of yarn

Waves crashing upon rocky shore and nearly engulfing lighthouse

Boy in short pants offering rose to blushing schoolgirl

Hausfrau triumphantly whisking fresh-baked muffins from glowing oven (beaming son in background)

Dapper middle-aged husband astounding frazzled wife with romantic kiss

Cheery, red-cheeked man hoisting beer stein at village festival

Crossing guard gaily halting traffic for mother and child

Skiff on placid lake, sunset

SOME FABRICATIONS TO INSERT INTO A PERSONAL DIARY

by Mike Sacks

Went to the moon today but came back in time for the PBS special on the origin of flight.

Invented a new use for the raisin.

Ran into George Clinton again. Nice guy.

Practiced the sitar for six hours on the roof. Hummingbird landed on my shoulder.

Swam the length of the Mississippi with a little help from a dolphin named Doug.

Almost ran for president. Made love to Shakira instead.

A UNICORN'S STRENGTHS

by Claire Zulkey

Medicinal horn

Flawless hair

Great handjobs

THINGS GOING THROUGH ROBERT PLANT'S MIND WHEN JIMMY PAGE TAKES A SOLO

by Ryan Boudinot

What is today, Wednesday?
It's been . . . What is it,
Tuesday . . . Monday . . .
I guess it really *has* been a
long time since I've rocked
and rolled.

And to think I spent the
whole bloody trilogy
thinking Golum was the
king. That he'd somehow
transform himself on Mount
Doom into, I don't know, an
elfin warlord or some shite.
What the hell is wrong
with me?

Pelvic thrust, *pelvic* thrust,
pelvic thrust.

You: bird in front row with
the gorgeous bazooms. Maybe
a leg quiver will catch your
eye. *Ooooh yeah-ee-yeah.*

Let's try to pronounce the "v"
in "love" this next time,
what do you say. Change it
up a bit.

Oh fucking hell, I think
Jonesey forgot to pack his
bloody recorder.

BUMP BUMP wheedly
deedly deedly DEE! BUMP
BUMP wha-wha weeeeer
do-de-doodly-deet-dee.
BUMP BUMP wha-weert
doort do duh dee deer.
Doot doot deet doot duh
deert dee!

On a scale of one to ten? Last
night's orgy?
Definitely three and a half.

FAILED YO' MAMA JOKES

by Pasha Malla

Yo' mama is as fat as my mama.

Hey, Pedro Almodóvar just made a new movie, and it's called *All About Yo' Mama,* and it's a real disappointment.

Have you seen *Throw Mama from the Train?* I'm not saying we should throw yo' mama from the train or anything, but Devito + Crystal − Mama = CLASSIC.

Yo' mama is very beautiful. Ha-ha, just kidding.

When yo' mama was born, the doctor slapped yo' grandmama, who was actually a wolf *dressed up* as yo' grandmama, i.e., ugly.

Some aliens showed up the other day at yo' mama's house and they were all, "Jesus, that's one scary-looking lady." And the alien named Jesus, who was their leader, said, "Hold me."

If you look up the word "mama" in the dictionary, there's a picture of yo' mama—no, wait. . . . Maybe there's a picture of a rhinoceros, and it says yo' mama's name underneath? In italics? Hold on, I got one: for "rhinoceros," it has a picture of yo' mama. With a horn. And those birds that live on rhinoceroses, rent free. Burn!

"I'm the closest thing to American royalty."
— PARIS HILTON

OTHER AMERICANS CLOSE TO ROYALTY

by Jonathan Shipley

Burger King	Ru Paul
Fresh Prince of Bel-Air	Dairy Queen
John Tesh	Prince
Queen Latifah	Alf

UNPOPULAR HALLOWEEN COSTUMES FOR 1957

by Jonathan Shipley

Sputnik	A black person
Allen Ginsberg's beard	Steve Allen
Hurricane Audrey	

CELEBRITIES WHOSE CAMEO APPEARANCES ON *THE FLINTSTONES* WOULD NOT DEMAND A NAME CHANGE

by Martin Bell

Alicia Silverstone	The Rock
Stone Phillips	Sharon Stone
Chris Rock	Rocco Baldelli
Kid Rock	Sen. Barack Obama

SEVEN THINGS MY THREE-YEAR-OLD SON WANTS TO DECORATE HIS NEW ROOM WITH, AFTER AGREEING ON A PIRATE THEME BUT THEN SEEING THE N.C. WYETH ILLUSTRATIONS FOR *TREASURE ISLAND*

by Oronte Churm

Sailing ships	Policemen
Treasure map	Firemen

Toasters

Black

Really, anything is fine, as
long as it's not pirates

MY REJECTED COOKING SHOW IDEAS

by Dan Kennedy

*Three-Hour Meals for Just
Under $400*

*Dinner, a Movie, and Passive-
Aggressive Advances*

*Ten-Minute Hotel Room Meals
for Lonely Travelers*

*Iron Chef Electric Hotplate
Challenge*

Shopliftin' with Stacey

Institutional Cook Showdown

WHAT I LIKE ABOUT YOU

by James Muldowney

You hold me tight.

You really know how
to dance.

You keep me warm at night.

You are whispering in
my ear.

You tell me all the things   Hey.
that I want to hear.

REASONS BLOGGERS HATE
THE MAINSTREAM MEDIA

by William Wolfe

The MSM is too liberal.   Bloggers got stood up at
                                 prom. By the MSM.

Professor always calls on the
MSM.

LEAST REPUTABLE CHARITIES

by Lucas Cox

Doctors Without Credentials   Save the Children
                                 (so we can feed them to the
                                 other children)
Habitat for Sean Hannity

Feed the Children
(to other children)

SOME ADDITIONAL POLAR AMBULATIONS

by Matt Wyatt

Hike of the narwhal

Evening stroll of the
snow geese

Treadmill of the lemmings

Line dance of the caribou

Pass completion of the
polar bear

Pole vault of the harp seals

Jog-a-thon of the musk ox

THE EXTENDED FAMILY OF COMEDIAN YAHOO SERIOUS

by Patrick Cassels

Ouch Comfortable

Whoa Bored

Cough Healthy

Boohoo Happy

Growl Docile

Eek Brave

Oops Infallible

Ha-ha Jaded

Yawn Flabbergasted

MUNICH is a lovable city, a quality to be ascribed to the proverbial "Gemütlichkeit" of the Bavarian character. Give the people their art, their music, their Carneval privileges (just restored) and — their beer, and they ask nothing more of life. This "joy of living" proves infectious and strangers linger gladly within the walls. All Munich is a vast Museum with interesting architectural monuments and picturesque corners at every turn. The Wagnerian performances at the Prince Regent Theatre are unsurpassable and these alone would make Munich the Mecca of music lovers. The wonderful panorama of the Bavarian Highlands stretches up to the very gates of munich, and luxurious motor busses carry tourists to the twin cities of Garmisch-Partenkirchen, to Oberammergau, the home of the Passion Play, and to the romantic castles built by Wagner's friend, the "mad king of Bavaria".

THINGS ALMOST AS MAGICAL AS A UNICORN

by Bob Shea

A magical horse (without horn)

A really, really good mime

That spray that took the smell out of the sofa

A talking frog with a pointy hat and some basic sleight-of-hand skills

A dancing goat

A rabbit's foot taped to a horseshoe

SEVEN THINGS TOTAL STRANGERS APPARENTLY THINK IT'S PERFECTLY APPROPRIATE TO SAY TO A WOMAN DISCREETLY BREAST-FEEDING IN PUBLIC

by Jessy Randall

"That's sick."

"Good for you!"

"I think that's quite unladylike."

"I remember nursing—it felt like a rat was gnawing on my breast."

"I breast-fed my kids until they were three!"

[In a doctor's office, with
finger quotes] "I know it's
'the most natural thing in
the world,' but here's a
blanket to help you
cover up."

"Yummy!"

DESSERTS TO AVOID AT LAST MEALS

by Mike Sacks

Death by chocolate

Hanging by a rainbow
assortment of sugar-free
sorbets

Shot through the heart with
a platter of honey-glazed
crullers

An ice cream cake from
Carvel in the shape of an
electric chair that tastes
suspiciously similar to that
other ice cream cake in the
shape of a whale

SUMMER MOVIES OTHER THAN *MARCH OF THE PENGUINS* CONSERVATIVES ARE RALLYING BEHIND

by Matt Loker

Charlie and the Chocolate Factory

The imaginative children's tale imparts the values of family togetherness, honesty, and avoiding premarital intercourse. "For example," writes James Dobson, "Violet gives in to the *temptation* of chewing gum, and becomes abnormally fat (representing pregnancy). The other three children similarly give in to *temptation,* and they all become dead (representing a social disease)."

Wedding Crashers

This bawdy comedy fits in neatly with conservative values, such as heterosexuality. "[Vince Vaughn and Owen Wilson] have sex with many, many women," observes syndicated radio host Michael Savage. "Homosexual men can't do that, on account of science."

Batman Begins

Bruce Wayne is the wealthy playboy son of an influential plutocrat. Later in life, he makes amends for his father by taking a lone-wolf-vigilante-justice approach to morally dubious acts of violence. Conservatives applaud the film's use of a tricked-out Hummer as the Batmobile, which was totally sweet.

The Dukes of Hazzard

Not once is the word "evolution" used in this movie. Many pundits proclaim this to be a tacit endorsement of intelligent design. "This is by far the best evidence yet," exclaims a joyous Pat Robertson on *The 700 Club.*

**Star Wars: Episode III—
Revenge of the Sith**
Presents strong direct evidence for Christianity, owing mostly to Natalie Portman, who must be an

angel. "Aw, shucks," says conservative talk-show host Sean Hannity, who sheepishly lowers his head and draws an arc in the dirt with his shoe.

Madagascar
No one is aborted in this movie.

SEVEN PEOPLE WHO ARE SCREWING UP MARSHVILLE, MASSACHUSETTS (POP. 2,384), AND FRANK ANDERSON IS NUMBER 3

by Ralph Gamelli

7. Stan Conley
A Marshville basher. Uses the phrase "hick town" a lot, but not in the friendly, self-deprecating way the rest of us do. Either work on your sarcasm, Stan, or get the hell out. No one's forcing you to live here.

6. Bob Hendricks
On 9/11, while a lot of us were watching the TV in Harvey's Bar, Bob remarked that he went to New York City once, as a kid. Everyone was paying too much attention to the TV to hear him, and he shut his mouth

quick when he realized what
he said. But I heard him.
And I haven't forgotten.

5. Andy Shaw
Went to the community
college over in Springdale for
a semester and a half before
flunking out and taking a
job at the hardware store.
Probably considers himself
one of the cultural elite.

4. Christopher
Redding
Gets mad when people call
him Chris.

3. Frank Anderson
Frank: Hey, do you mind if I
borrow your shovel?

Me: Help yourself. It's in the
garage.

Frank: Thanks.

Frank has not returned this
shovel, and this shovel is a
good shovel and I want it in
my garage.

2. Burt Summers
Quit playing bocce; said the
shoes hurt his shins. He
could still come to the court
and cheer us on, but instead
he stays home and reads.
Books!

1. Mike Morgan
Too close for comfort.

REJECTED SUBMISSIONS FOR STARBUCKS' "THE WAY I SEE IT"

by Tim Williams

Wouldn't it be nice if, instead of a "double shot of espresso," you could pound a couple jiggers of rye into this coffee? Then go back to work and pimp slap the boss? Yeah, that'd be great. Not gonna happen, though, fella. You'll finish your pastry, grit your teeth, and get back to the grind. Bottoms up!

Boobs, hooters, headlights, fun bags, party girls— society has made great strides, but in the matter of synonyms for "breasts," it really doesn't get any better than "tits."

The way I see it, Lloyd is crazy. Not just short-pants-in-winter kinda crazy but batshit kinda crazy. Wears-a-velvet-cape-to-get-to-the-mail kinda crazy. Eats-imaginary-ice-cream-cone-while-talking-to-the-ghost-of-his-long-dead-Aunt-Hettie kinda crazy. Doesn't mean he shouldn't be allowed to drive a bus, though. It's just the way I see it.

People, in general, lack perspective. I say everyone should have to busk out on a street corner or in a public market at least twice a year. Not necessarily playing Neil Young tunes on the guitar, either. Do your job, for change, in front of the 17th Avenue liquor store. Then go back to work and complain about having to share an office.

Be the person you always wanted to be. Do it now. Especially if the person you want to be is the sort who knocks over shelves and merchandise displays in a coffee shop while giving strangers wedgies and singing "Forget your troubles, c'mon get happy!"

Okay, so they've got Alcoholics Anonymous, and Narcotics Anonymous, and Gamblers Anonymous. In fact, there are well over a hundred twelve-step anonymous-type programs. So how come there's no Useless-Twat-Who-Lives-Upstairs-from-Me-Who-Insists-on-Playing-Dance-Music-Early-Sunday-Morning Anonymous?

If you love someone, set him free. If he comes back, make sure you get the money he owes from before you set him free.

THIRTY-NINE QUESTIONS FOR CHARLIE DANIELS UPON HEARING "THE DEVIL WENT DOWN TO GEORGIA" FOR THE FIRST TIME IN TWENTY-FIVE YEARS

by John Moe

1. The devil won that fiddling contest, right?

2. Because isn't that totally amazing fiddle-feedback thing the devil plays (which sounds like Hendrix gone bluegrass) a hundred times better than that high-school-band piece-of-crap tune Johnny plays?

3. I mean, come on, right?

4. And since the devil is so clearly better, why does he lay the golden fiddle on the ground at Johnny's feet?

5. What kind of one-sided bet was that anyway, your eternal soul for a fiddle?

6. Shouldn't it have been something like Johnny's soul or the eradication of evil?

7. Or maybe a golden fiddle against some object Johnny placed great value upon?

8. If the devil went down to Georgia 'cause he was looking for a soul to *steal,* why does he arrange what appears to be an honest competition?

9. Was there actually some hidden theft or scam going on here on the part of the devil?

10. Then why not explain that, Mr. Daniels?

11. And who was judging that contest?

12. Was it an honor-system kind of thing?

13. With the devil?

14. Honor system with the devil. How did Johnny get sucked into that one?

15. Does Johnny suffer from some—I'm trying to be delicate here—cognitive disabilities?

16. Was there some sort of arbitration board in place in the event that the outcome was not obvious?

17. If so, who served on this board?

18. It wasn't the demons, was it?

19. 'Cause even though they're the only characters in the song, they're kind of biased since they're in the devil's band and they're demons, right?

20. So why—*why*—does the devil take the dive and throw the contest?!

21. I mean, the devil can't be hurting for cash. How much is it going to cost him to buy a new golden fiddle?

22. I'm thinking maybe $18,000. Does that sound right to you?

23. If you're Johnny, what do you even want with a golden fiddle?

24. Doesn't the metallic surface of a golden fiddle create an unpalatably tinny sound as opposed to the nice resonant sound from a wooden instrument?

25. Does he think he's going to display it in his home and tell people the story of how he beat the devil?

26. Who's going to believe that?

27. Or does he try to sell the fiddle?

28. If so, how does he go about getting something like that appraised?

29. Or does he just melt it all down for the gold?

30. That sounds awfully hard, don't you think?

31. And is Johnny haunted by the question of why the devil let him win like that?

32. Was there some catch in the contest that Johnny wasn't aware of where the devil really does get his soul anyway and Johnny didn't

notice it because he's not all that smart?

33. And even if he didn't get Johnny's soul, what is Johnny going to say to God in heaven when he has to explain that he bet his soul, the essence of life, God's one true gift, on a fiddling contest?

34. Johnny knows deep down that he's not really the best that's ever been and that's the source of his insecure boasting, right?

35. Was it really necessary or wise to invite the devil to come on back if he ever wants to try again?

36. 'Cause what does Johnny need, a *second* golden fiddle?

37. Or maybe a golden viola the next time?

38. Why would the devil need an invitation?

39. Are you implying, Mr. Daniels, that Johnny actually wants to get hustled?

ANTICLIMACTIC *TWILIGHT ZONE* EPISODES

by Jim Stallard

"The Garden"

A spaceship crash-lands on an unknown planet. The two surviving astronauts, a man and a woman, realize the spaceship is damaged beyond repair and that it will be impossible for anyone to come rescue them. They find they are able to live easily off the bountiful vegetation, which provides everything they need—indeed, the setting turns out to be idyllic. Eventually, they start a family on their new planet. This couple becomes known to later generations as . . . Richard Benson and Margaret Wilson, crew members on NASA's lost *Voyager* mission, which disappeared after failing to follow proper emergency procedures.

"Time Enough at Last"
A humble bank clerk bemoans the hectic pace of his life because it limits the time he gets to spend with his books. After an H-bomb attack, the clerk emerges from a bank vault to learn that everyone else on Earth has perished. The man becomes ecstatic when he realizes he finally can read as much as he likes. Later, however, he finds he must spend a lot more time foraging for food than he expected, and at the end of the day he just wants to

sleep, so the whole thing is a bit of a washout.

"The Eye of the Beholder"
A young woman, her head wrapped in bandages, waits for the results of a desperate operation to alter her disfigured face; if the surgery has failed, she will be sent to a colony of freaks. Throughout the episode, the viewer hears the voices of the doctors and family members but never sees their faces. When the bandages are finally removed, they reveal a plain-faced woman with several visible scars. The woman's father says the surgeon probably did the best he could under the circumstances and sends his daughter to Sarah Lawrence.

"Where Is Everybody?"
A man emerges from his office to find the hallways mysteriously devoid of coworkers. He wanders the silent, empty building looking for signs of life but

finds no trace of humanity other than coffee brewing, purses slung over chairs, and folders lying open on desks. Suddenly he remembers a mandatory meeting in the first-floor conference room.

"The Monsters Are Due on Maple Street"

After sighting an unusual meteor overhead, suburban residents become increasingly paranoid when their electric power suddenly fails to function. As the tension mounts, the neighbors begin to suspect one another of being disguised aliens who caused the mysterious outage, and they make wild accusations and attack one another. Then one man hears on his radio that the blackout was caused by a Texas-based energy company that manipulated the power grid. The residents become outraged over this for a few days and then fixate on property taxes.

"Ghost War"

Three national guardsmen stationed near the site of Custer's Last Stand find themselves snared in the chaos of the Battle of Little Big Horn. After the men radio for help, the cowboys and Indians are forcibly removed and security is beefed up in the area.

"Finding the Key"

A once-successful songwriter, frustrated by severe creative block, meets a mysterious old Chinese man hawking his wares in a downtown flea market. The man sells him a token that will supposedly restore his lost gift for music. The next day, the songwriter sits down at the piano and writes "My Ding-a-Ling."

YOU MIGHT BE A REDNECK . . .

by Trevor Seigler

If you go out in the sun without wearing sunscreen and you absorb a lot of solar radiation on the back of your neck, you might be a redneck

If you get in a tanning bed and come out with sunburn on your body 'cause you didn't use enough sunblock, chances are you might be a redneck

If you listen to country music and fly a rebel flag everywhere you go and your neck gets burned from exposure to the sun when you're out partying with friends while Hank Junior blares in the background, you might be a redneck

If you have to clean off the roof of your trailer on a hot summer day and you take off your shirt under the hot sun, you might be a redneck

If you stay out in the sun so long that you contract skin cancer and die, you might be a redneck

If you tell lame jokes about how "you might be a redneck" for well over a decade and no one wants to hear your newer material, you might be wondering where it all went wrong by now

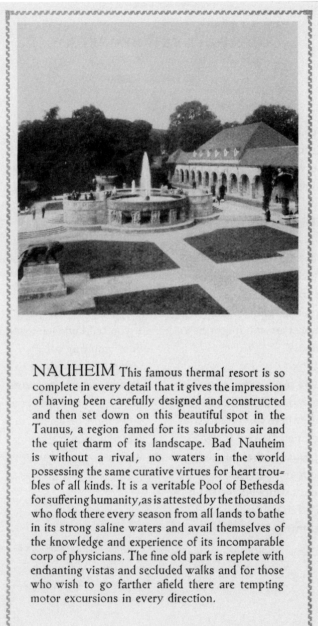

NAUHEIM This famous thermal resort is so complete in every detail that it gives the impression of having been carefully designed and constructed and then set down on this beautiful spot in the Taunus, a region famed for its salubrious air and the quiet charm of its landscape. Bad Nauheim is without a rival, no waters in the world possessing the same curative virtues for heart troubles of all kinds. It is a veritable Pool of Bethesda for suffering humanity, as is attested by the thousands who flock there every season from all lands to bathe in its strong saline waters and avail themselves of the knowledge and experience of its incomparable corp of physicians. The fine old park is replete with enchanting vistas and secluded walks and for those who wish to go farther afield there are tempting motor excursions in every direction.

WORLD-HISTORICAL CHENEYS

by Benjamin Cohen

"I think they're in the last throes, if you will, of the insurgency."
—DICK CHENEY (2005, on *Larry King Live*)

Japanese Cheney-San,
1945, Nagasaki
"People, uh, listen, people.
I think the dignity-hating
radioactive menace raining
down and through us is in
the last throes, if you will, of
obliterating us."

Passenger-Pigeon Cheney,
1899, Ohio
"Seriously, Britt, these flight-
hating humans are done.
We've beaten them back. It's
over, adios, sayonara, things
are on the up and up from
here on out, away from the
fashionable hats and back to
blackening the sky with our
masses."

Aztec Cheney,
1519, Teotihuacán
"Stick a fork in 'em, Larry.
With Quetzalcoatl and our
freedom-loving cannibalism
behind us, I can tell you
that, errrr, Cortés is in the
last throes of this meek geno-
cide."

**Roman Theodosius
Cheney,**
455, Rome
"Laughable, Hannityus,
laughable. Goths, shmoths,
these insurgents. They *es in
sum permaneo per.*"

**The Last Oreos in the
Bag Cheney,**
1987, Kroger
"That pathetic kid, I see his
face, and I'm looking at our
double-stuffed intelligence,
and I can say those teeth are
in their last throes . . . everything's gonna be fine. That
big glass of 2 percent grade
A will be the dunking of victory!"

The Cheney X7G-iiC,
2253, Ameri-World
"Larry, I'm sitting here—
well, bolted here, heh-heh—
and the way we're looking at
this, the swarming billions
upon billions of freedom-
hating Seyfert Type-II galaxy
M77 insurgents are in their
last throes. From here in my
escape pod, I can see that this
moment of total apocalyptic
horror is just about past.
These are aliens who disagree
with our policies, our ways of
programming. You'll always
have the naysayers. It's us or
them, Larry 2Xiv-Q."

THE GAY AGENDA

by L.

7:45 A.M. Alarm rings

8:00–8:10 A.M. Take shower

8:15–8:30 A.M. Dress and
put items into briefcase

8:35 A.M. Leave house

8:45 A.M. Starbucks

9:00 A.M. Arrive at job

12:00 P.M. Lunch with a coworker. Chili's?

12:45 P.M. Return to job

1:30–2:30 P.M. Meeting

5:00 P.M. Leave work

5:30–6:30 P.M. Work out in gym

7:00 P.M. Return home

7:20 P.M. Prepare and eat dinner

8:00 P.M. Watch *Law & Order* on TNT

11:00 P.M. Go to sleep

HOW TO TELL IF A UNICORN IS INTO YOU

by Elizabeth Ellen

He pays for dinner.

He tells you repeatedly you have beautiful eyes.

He sends you flowers when it isn't your birthday or Valentine's Day.

HOW TO TELL IF A UNICORN JUST ISN'T THAT INTO YOU

by Elizabeth Ellen

He says he'll call but he doesn't.

He tells you he's gay.

You overhear him telling your coworkers you're "just friends."

NICKNAMES I WOULD GIVE MY PENIS IF I WERE IN THE MOB

by Mike Sacks

Little Mike

Mikey Jr.

"The Penis" Sacks

BAD NAME FOR HELICOPTER CHARTER COMPANY

by Dan Kennedy

Captain Swervy's

CHANGES TO THE HOTEL CALIFORNIA MADE IN RESPONSE TO MR. HENLEY'S RECENT COMPLAINT

by John Moe

Update room decor, including removal of ceiling mirrors

Restock spirit supplies, encourage captain to offer guests other options

Acquire steelier knives and/or less resolute beast

Emphasize "heaven" image over less desirable "hell" alternative

Install electric-light system in hallway (long overdue), reassign employee who has been showing guests to room by candlelight

Upgrade music selection to accommodate both guests who dance to remember and those who do so to forget

Improve courtyard air-conditioning to reduce occurrences of sweet summer sweat

Encourage nightman to be
less cryptic when talking to
guests

Reduce power on colitas-oil
highway pumps; smell may
be overly aggressive

Clearly mark passage back to
places guests have been
before

Provide house alibis to
guests who neglect to bring
their own

Emphasize core strengths:
lovely place, plenty of room,
consistent location

Streamline checkout

OPENING LINES TO THE ROUGH DRAFT
OF RUDYARD KIPLING'S "IF"

by Mike Sacks

IF you can keep your head
when all about you
Are losing theirs
Are losing theirs

IF you can keep your head
when, when, when,
?
Goddamnit.

Are
?
Shit.

IF you can keep your head
when all about you, when all
about you, when, if you can,
if, all about you, Christ
damn, screw it.

SOME OF THE PEOPLE WHO HAVE CONTACTED ME SINCE I RECEIVED A MACARTHUR GRANT LAST WEEK, WHO PROBABLY WOULD NOT HAVE CONTACTED ME OTHERWISE

by Emily Thompson

My Governor, Arnold Schwarzenegger

A guy I wanted to have sex with last year, who neglected to return my calls at that time

A guy in a band that I really need to hear

A guy making a documentary that I really need to see

A guy who just really thinks we need to talk

An old man who just wants to be sure that I drive carefully

Another guy I wanted to have sex with last year, who resisted my attentions and overtures at that time

The chancellor of the university at which I teach

An old man who just wanted to tell me a story about how the actor Andy Devine couldn't find work when sound movies came in because of his high squeaky voice so he tried to gas himself to death but he hadn't paid his bill so the gas company turned off the gas so he didn't die and then there was a knock on his door and it was someone offering a job in a movie and he soon thereafter became rich and famous because of his high squeaky voice

A very old man who, as a nine-month-old baby, appeared in a Lon Chaney silent movie

The guy I really wanted to have sex with last year, who failed to succumb to my feminine charms at that time

WAYS TO SALUTE THOSE ABOUT TO ROCK

by Lauren Oster

Organize parade

Declare bank holiday

Rename specialty pizza

Show tits

Produce biopic

Issue commemorative coin

PUNCH LINES TO JOKES UNICORNS LIKE TO TELL ABOUT THE IRISH

by Carlton Doby

"Thirty-five? And he still believes in leprechauns?"

"I don't know, Seamus. I wonder if we're t'rowin' the dog high enough."

"Aye laddie, and their boat's for sale."

A little embarrassed, the golfer says to the leprechaun,

"Well, that's not too bad for a Catholic priest in a small parish."

THINGS MY BOSS HAS SAID TO UNCOMFORTABLY INSERT ME INTO HIS PERSONAL LIFE

by John Shortino

"Incidentally, that was the same woman who stabbed me."

"And I told my son, you have to clean your ass once, maybe twice a day. Otherwise they'll call you 'stinky.' "

"When I was in college, I was . . . I don't know, a freak is the wrong word. Would 'slut' be the right word for a

man? Well, I was something like that."

"When my roommate was coming back, he had a motorcycle accident . . . slid right across the gas tank . . . cut up all over . . . he *ripped his testicles off.*"

"By the way, you may see me wearing sunglasses all the time. It's because I am blind

in one eye, and there is
extensive scarring. This is all
a result of diabetes."

"I ended up having to tackle
her into a wall. I broke three
of her ribs."

IF YOU SHOULD ENCOUNTER
A DIAMONDBACK RATTLESNAKE
WHILE HIKING

by Dan Kennedy

Cover arms in makeshift
armor consisting of shag
carpet scraps and duct tape.

Put on cobra mask.

Speak loudly and confidently
of having taken larger prey as
a cobra than a diamondback
rattlesnake could ever take.

When speaking, use the
word "shit" in place of the
word "stuff" or "things" and
end sentences with "man."

Use arms to move
diamondback rattlesnake

over a few feet from where it
is currently coiled in your
path.

Next, look at diamondback
rattlesnake as if you're still
not happy with him being
even anywhere near your
path, then move snake an
additional three to five yards
away.

Start returning to path in
order to resume hike,
stopping midway back to
turn around and say,
"What'd you just say to me?
[Hold it for a beat.] Just say

it again if you want up to an ounce of cobra venom in your blood. [Hold it for a beat again.] Yeah, I didn't think so."

Resume hiking, being sure to mention to any other hiker(s) you encounter on the path the general area the diamondback rattlesnake was first encountered and how far off the path it was relocated.

Remove cobra mask and makeshift armor, offering them to hiker(s) if they plan on passing through that area.

MY MOTHER HAS NOT YET GOTTEN THE HANG OF TEXT MESSAGING

by Kyle BaShaw

"I am late. I used my whmmmmmle lunachill be there at"

"h"

"on MY WAYYTO WORK"

". "

"Happy Birthday"
(two months later)

TAKING A RUSH LIMBAUGH QUOTE FROM WWW.BRAINYQUOTE.COM, TRANSLATING IT INTO SPANISH AND THEN BACK TO ENGLISH USING BABELFISH AND WINDING UP WITH WHAT APPEARS TO BE A STATE ADDRESS BY A LOCAL GOVERNMENT OFFICIAL TRYING TO QUELL A MINOR INSURRECTION IN A SMALL GERMAN TOWN CIRCA 1752 AD

by Jerry Minihane

"The uproars of the Angels were not caused
by the verdict of the king of Rodney. The uproars of the Angels
were caused by rioters."

NAMES OF JAPANESE COIN-OP MAHJONG VIDEO GAMES THAT HAVE A SEXUAL THEME EITHER REAL OR IMAGINED

by Mike Scullen

Bishoujo Janshi Pretty Sailor

City Love

Crystal Gal

Disco Mahjong Otachidai no Okite

House Mannequin Roppongi Live

Idol-Mahjong Final Romance

Jyanshin Densetsu—Quest of Jongmaster

Lovely Pop Mahjong Jan Jan Simasyo

Mahjong Banana Dream

Mahjong Camera Kozou

Mahjong Clinic

Mahjong Diplomat

Mahjong Erotica Golf

Mahjong Hyper Reaction

Mahjong Koi no Magic Potion

Mahjong the Lady Hunter

Pastel Gal

Scandal Mahjong

Super Real Mahjong Part 3

Taisen Hot Gimmick

Telephone Mahjong

ALTERNATE NAMES FOR "I CAN'T BELIEVE IT'S NOT BUTTER" SPREAD

by Bob Shea

"Not butter? Then what the hell did I just eat?" spread

"I still say it's butter" spread

"After all the damage you've done to this family with your habitual lying and deceit, you have the nerve to sit there with a straight face and tell me that this isn't butter?" spread

"I'm pretty sure that was butter" spread

"I'm comfortable calling this butter" spread

"This challenges everything I've come to believe about butter" spread

"I'm not entirely sure it's edible" spread

"I'm willing to suspend disbelief about this being butter for about as long as it takes me to eat this toast" spread

"In the absence of actual butter, sure, I'll play along" spread

"I guess you could call it butter. If you don't put any in your mouth" spread

"I can't believe it's so flammable" spread

"Am I wrong about God too?" spread

NUREMBERG owes its perennial popularity
to its Old World atmosphere, to the impressive
picturesqueness of its medieval architecture, and
to the enduring monuments of iron and stone, of
song and story, of the brush and the pen left by
such masters as Albrecht Dürer, Hans Sachs, Me-
lanchthon, Peter Vischer, Veit Stoss, Adam Krafft,
and an illustrious line of craftsmen who lived at a
time in the world's history when men "worked for
the joy of the working!" In the Germanic Museum,
the history of German civilization may be traced
as clearly as if one were turning the pages of volume
of old prints. The visitor wanders about enchanted
among the churches, richly-wrought fountains, and
palaces of the erstwhile Nuremberg patricians, and
then up the hill to the old fortress crowning the
summit, there to look out over the "sea of roofs"
and drink in the beauty of the mise, en-scene.

FILMS TO MAKE BEFORE HARVEY KORMAN AND TIM CONWAY BECOME TOO FEEBLE

by Charlie Hopper

Bonnie's Ancient Shuffling Doctor and Clyde

Butch Cassidy and the Guy Who Makes Him Giggle Unprofessionally

Harold and Kumar Go to Sunday Brunch Buffet at the Sheraton

UNICORNS ARE BETTER THAN CATS BECAUSE . . .

by Mike Sacks

Unicorns are like males. They wake up late, don't need much in the way of attention, and urinate standing up.

Unicorns can be trained, whereas you could never in a million years train a cat to fly you to a magical fantasy kingdom on its back.

Cats look silly posing under rainbows.

REASONS IT WOULD BE COOL TO BE FRIENDS WITH GEORGE W. BUSH

by Jeremy A. Cohen

Sleepovers at the White House

Late night snacks prepared by White House chef during sleepovers at White House

Making elaborate fort out of blankets and pillows in Lincoln Bedroom, then attacking and/or defending it with G.I. Joe and Cobra action figures during sleepovers at White House

Would give me an affectionate nickname— perhaps "J-Man" or "Skippy"

Possibility of lifetime appointment to one of the most important jobs in the country despite no discernible qualifications for that job

THINGS THAT CAN BEAT ROCK, PAPER, AND SCISSORS

by Dan Levine

Heroism

Storm surge

Wet-dry Shop-Vac

Pressure

Blind drunken rage

Lava

Teamwork

Love

Double amputation

POSSIBLE FUTURE *LAST ANGRY MAN* ROLES FOR RUSSELL CROWE

by Alex Zuckerman

Former Baltimore Orioles
manager Earl Weaver

Suge Knight

Star Trek XI villain whose
inner beauty has been
destroyed and yearns to be
understood on his own
authoritarian terms

Cato the *Elder*

Roman Polanski

Friedrich Nietzsche

B2604-79/Q

Macbeth in version of
Macbeth set in Ireland instead
of Scotland

POLITELY NEUTRAL BLURBS FOR THE DUST JACKETS OF BOOKS I WAS SENT BY PUBLISHERS AND DIDN'T REALLY CARE FOR

by Dan Kennedy

"It's different. I mean it's just . . . different. Which is fine."

"I'll tell you what, I sure love reading in general."

"Available now in hardcover, and I wouldn't be surprised to see it get put out in paperback sometime next year."

"Oh, honestly . . . I don't know. Really, what do I know? Don't listen to me."

HOUSING DEVELOPMENT NAMES THAT SOUND LIKE PORN STAR NAMES

by Michael Patrick Sullivan

Tiffany Oaks

Misty Woods

Lorelei Chase

Peach Hills

Bristle Valley

Lilith Greens

Palomino Fields   Jameson Hole

Glen Everwood

THE WEEK AHEAD: FIVE-WORD VERIFICATION STRINGS TO WATCH FOR

by Tom Peyer

1. ewbbcxe   4. svwxxszg

2. vgyek   5. uyzpyko

3. yozatym

THE MOST COMMONLY USED INTERJECTIONS, ACCORDING TO THE THIRD EDITION OF *ESSENTIALS OF ENGLISH GRAMMAR*

by Lindsay Knight

Ah   Congratulations

Alas   Good grief

Great	No
Help	No way
Hey	Oh
Hooray	Ouch
Hurry	Outstanding
My goodness	Ugh
Never	Wow

PROFESSIONAL WRESTLER?
OR SONG BY CAPTAIN BEEFHEART?

by Joe Lex

1. 1-2-3 Kid
2. 25th Century Quaker
3. Abba Zaba
4. American Avalanche
5. Amish Roadkill
6. Bad News Brown
7. Bastian Booger
8. Big Eyed Beans
9. Dingo Warrior
10. Dirty Blue Gene

11. Doctor Dark

12. Doctor Death

13. Flash Funk

14. Funeral Hill

15. Headbanger Mosh

16. Koko B. Ware

17. Mirror Man

18. Moondog Spot

19. Orange Claw Hammer

20. Pachuco Cadaver

21. Pompadour Swamp

22. Psycho Sid

23. Sheriff of Hong Kong

24. Starship Coyote

25. Sue Egypt

26. Sugar 'N Spikes

27. Tiger Mask

28. White Jam

ANSWERS

Beefheart: 2, 3, 8, 10, 11, 14, 17, 19, 20, 21, 23, 25, 26, 28

Wrestler: 1, 4, 5, 6, 7, 9, 12, 13, 15, 16, 18, 22, 24, 27

CIRCUMSTANCES THAT WOULD JUSTIFY MY NEXT-DOOR NEIGHBOR'S RECENT ACQUISITION OF A MCHBX 20 VANITY PLATE

by Kristen Roupenian and Hanlon Smith–Dorsey

My neighbor, an aficionado of pre-Vietnam-era diner memorabilia, has, after a long and bitter search, finally managed to lay his hand on the "Harvest House Cafeterias and Coffee Shops" limited issue matchbox of 1961, thereby bringing the number of items in his matchbox collection to, you guessed it, twenty.

My neighbor is Rob Thomas.

SUPERHERO POWERS RECOVERED FROM THE CUTTING ROOM FLOOR

by Franco Fiorini

Random vomiting

The knack of continually being mistaken for the party girl from college

The power to attract over-forty, balding, and close-talking town drunks

The ability to send yourself directly to hell

THINGS IN THE EYE OF THE BEHOLDER

by Bobby Foley

Beauty

Truth

The contact lens of the
beholder

RELATIONSHIP SKILLS I LEARNED FROM READING *BLACK'S LAW DICTIONARY,* 2ND POCKET EDITION

by Zack Schwartz and Katherine Sharpe

Responsive pleading

Accusatory pleading

Anomalous pleading

Articulated pleading

Shotgun pleading

Artful pleading

Plea of tender

THINGS DAKOTA FANNING COULD SAY THAT WOULD MAKE ME SMILE

by Justin Paul Villegas

"Excuse me please mister?"

"YUM! Grape juice!"

"Rain, rain go away!"

"Karl Rove—what a cocksucker."

BAD WORDS AND PHRASES FOR IMPROV COMEDY TROUPES TO ACCEPT FROM THE AUDIENCE IN ORDER TO START THE SHOW

by Dan Kennedy

Rodomontade

Muntjac

Hod

"Doko no gakkou-ni itte imasu-ka?"

ART GARFUNKEL, TELEVISION GUEST STAR

by John Moe

American Idol
(season one)
Kelly Clarkson falls in love
with Garfunkel, who is
employed as a backstage
adviser to contestants.
Distracted by the crush, she
loses contest. Vastly inferior
Justin Guarini, possessed of
vaguely Garfunkelesque
hairdo, wins.

Law & Order
Through a series of free
concerts in the park,
Garfunkel overcomes crime
in the city of New York as
criminals are persuaded by
his beautiful high tenor to
end their deviant ways. Cast
spends most of the time
doing crossword puzzles.

World News Tonight
Viewers are uncomfortable
with Garfunkel's looming
background presence as he
waits to join Peter Jennings
for "the high parts" of
the newscast, which never
arrive.

Little House on the Prairie
As Pa's long-lost troubadour
brother "Arthur," Garfunkel
drives action to a halt
with twice-per-show
performances. Worse, all
songs are old Simon and
Garfunkel numbers with
Garfunkel singing only his
own parts, followed by angry
obscenity-laced tirades about
former partner.

The X-Files
Investigations are derailed as
Special Agent Garfunkel
demands Mulder and Scully
investigate Paul Simon's
potential involvement in
every single case. When
Simon is always proven to
have an alibi, Garfunkel

seethes, "He got away this time."

Muppet Babies

In the presence of full-grown nonanimated Garfunkel, who appears to have no real dramatic function, visibly frightened Muppet babies retreat into their own private worlds, never have any adventures, never say anything cute or clever, and become very lonely.

Fantasy Island

Playing himself, Garfunkel appears in each show's opening sequence. Mr. Roarke asks all guests if any of their fantasies involve Art Garfunkel. They always say no, so Garfunkel spends the rest of the episode wandering around the island and mooching food.

The Golden Girls

Garfunkel plays Bea Arthur's down-on-his-luck nephew who comes to live with the ladies. Once there, he never really does anything but sit on the couch sighing. All characters lose their zest for life and soon die of natural causes.

COUNTRIES THAT PEOPLE THINK MY DUTCH GIRLFRIEND NAMED NOOR COMES FROM, EVEN AFTER BEING TOLD THAT SHE IS DUTCH

by John Miller

Norway

Countries that I imagine the same people must think I come from:

Jonway

Jonland

Jonalia

Jonistan

Jonesia

Equatorial John

Papua New John

REJECTED LYRICS FOR THE KILLERS' "ALL THESE THINGS THAT I'VE DONE" BEFORE THEY EVENTUALLY SETTLED ON "I'VE GOT SOUL, BUT I'M NOT A SOLDIER"

by Beth Edwards

I've got fat, but I'm not a father.

I've got a coat, but I'm not a coatrack.

I've got heat, but I'm not a heathen.

I've got a cat, but I'm really more of a dog person.

I've got ambition, but I'm not one of those people who's just going to knock everyone out of his way to get what he wants, you know?

I've got a rash, but I don't think it's contagious.

I've got cocaine, but I'm just holding it for a friend.

I've got some David Bowie CDs, but I'm no David Bowie.

HAIRCUTS I HAVE REVIEWED WHILE RIDING TO WORK ON THE SUBWAY

by Sarah Mi Ra Dougherty

On a bowl cut:
"This cut is to fashion sense what the microwave is to cooking: bland, insipid, and uninspired."

On a bob:
"Great energy but poor execution."

On a crew cut:
"A minefield of danger and delight. The gel says 'stay' and the spikes say 'play.' "

On a double French braid:
"This casual luxury brings to mind Heidi of the Swiss prom."

On a short cut (male):
"Wind-tossed fun—the
happy drama of the ocean
played out on the surface of a
human head."

On a short cut (female):
"A short, shorn bird's nest of
salt-and-pepper
respectability. Middle-aged
never had it so good."

On a hat:
"A triumph of
understatement."

THINGS I HATE MOST
ABOUT BEING A SLAVE TO THE ROBOTS

by Christopher Monks

Getting electrocuted for
looking directly into their
ocular tubes

Cleaning the bathroom

My polyester slave jerkin

Getting electrocuted for nodding off during robot opera

Limited access to my blog

Robot night terrors

Getting electrocuted for not
greasing Lord Zelchron's
knobs adequately

Lousy dental coverage

Not getting Columbus Day
off

Getting electrocuted for
forgetting to record *Extreme
Makeover: Robot Domicile
Edition*

Getting electrocuted for sighing	No one ever saying thank you
	All the electrocuting

NOTABLE BANDS OF 2005

by Ed Page

Rubber

Head

Wrist

Hat

AMENDED TAGLINES FOR ARBY'S

by Dan Kennedy

I'm thinking Arby's. . . . I'm also thinking it's three in the morning, we've been drinking, and we both have to work tomorrow.

I'm thinking Arby's . . . that said, I'm the same guy who was thinking we wouldn't get caught sneaking into the Radiohead concert, and that didn't pan out real well.

I'm thinking Arby's. . . . but then again spending three hours driving in bad weather was also my idea.

PRENUDE SUN BED–USE CHECKLIST

by Roy Kesey

Door closed

Door locked

Security camera covered with spare T-shirt

Magazine close at hand

Music selection adequate

Tiny alien beings

Butt cheeks spread slightly to avoid weird white circle

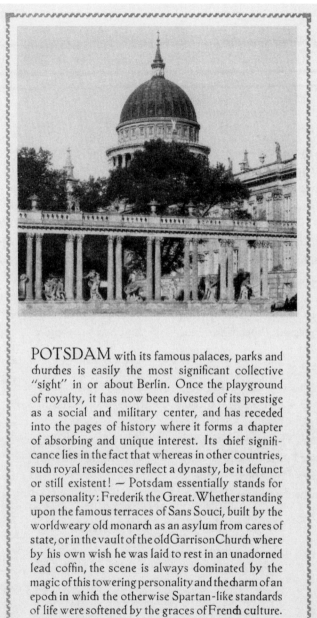

POTSDAM with its famous palaces, parks and churches is easily the most significant collective "sight" in or about Berlin. Once the playground of royalty, it has now been divested of its prestige as a social and military center, and has receded into the pages of history where it forms a chapter of absorbing and unique interest. Its chief significance lies in the fact that whereas in other countries, such royal residences reflect a dynasty, be it defunct or still existent! — Potsdam essentially stands for a personality: Frederik the Great. Whether standing upon the famous terraces of Sans Souci, built by the worldweary old monarch as an asylum from cares of state, or in the vault of the old Garrison Church where by his own wish he was laid to rest in an unadorned lead coffin, the scene is always dominated by the magic of this towering personality and the charm of an epoch in which the otherwise Spartan-like standards of life were softened by the graces of French culture.

OVERHEARD ON THE DAY
THEY INVENTED SLICED BREAD

by Pasha Malla

"Wow, this is—*man,* this is just so great. I can't even think of anything to compare this to."

"Holy. Fucking. Shit. Are you kidding me with this stuff?"

"You know, I'm just not that impressed. I mean, you hear all the hype, how everyone's talking, 'Oh, you've got to see this new thing they're doing with bread!' and you think, 'Okay, sure, I'll give it a shot, I'm not some bread snob, I'm willing to try new things.' But, now? Sitting here with it right in front of me? I honestly can't say— and I'm sorry for this, I hope I'm not offending anyone— that I'm that blown away. Looks just like a regular old loaf of bread to me. [. . .] Oh, wait. *Hold on a goddamn minute!* Would you look at that. They just went ahead and cut *right the way through!* And here's one piece . . . and look, another! And another and *another*—amazing, simply amazing! Who did this? Who is the *culinary genius* behind this?! I take it all back. My bad, guys. You were right. My bad."

"Yum."

THINGS YOU DON'T EXPECT TO READ ON THE FLYER PINNED TO YOUR NEIGHBORHOOD TELEPHONE POLE

by Jonathan Shipley

FOUND—Telephone pole

Garage Sale Saturday
(10′ × 20′)

CAR WASH—to benefit
Brown Bear Car Wash

PLACES YOU'RE LIKELY TO FIND A UNICORN

by Patrick Cassels

The time before time

The Third Age

Where Pan doth play his pipes

Realms of wizardry, necromancy, and general enchantment

New Zealand

Trapper Keepers

JESUS OF NAZARETH'S ROUGH DRAFTS

by Sean Carman

Let him who is without fault see if he can do any better.

Blessed are the meek—they are the politest people anywhere.

It is easier for a rich man to enter the kingdom of heaven than for a camel to pass through [something really tiny here that a camel could never pass through . . . I don't know . . . a link in a chain, maybe? An earring? A flute?]

You are the salt of the earth. But if salt has lost its taste, how shall its saltness be restored? By "saltness" I mean the thing that makes it salty. Whatever essential quality makes it salt. That is what I mean by "saltness." Where was I?

This bread is like me, but not like me. You know what I mean. Same goes for the wine.

You are the light of the world. A city set on a hill cannot be hid. You're like a house on fire. You're burning up. Look at you go!

Forgive them Father, they're trying their best.

UNSATISFACTORY REASONS TO RESUME MANNED FLIGHTS TO THE MOON

by Ed Page

To correct typo on moon plaque

Billions of dollars burning a hole in your pocket

TASKS I'M NOT TOO EMBARRASSED TO HAVE MY HELPER MONKEY PERFORM

by Mike Sacks

My taxes

Telling my wife that I don't love her anymore, or at least not as much as I used to

Calling my doctor to make an appointment for the itching and the rash that can't quite be diagnosed from a quick search during lunch hour on the public library's computer

Attending the funeral of my ex-best friend from college, the one who didn't talk to me for years because I never sent him a card when he was sick with cancer for the first time

Clipping my grandmother's toenails while listening to her make racist small talk about various minorities, including Haitian-Americans, as her Haitian-

American caregiver sits behind us reading an old issue of *Smithsonian*

Buying the marked-down condoms at the dollar store, the ones that are perfectly safe, just a little generic looking. Then having intercourse with the woman I recently met on the Internet

Making the monkey bastard drive himself back to the pet store to get a refund. About two hours later I'll stop by the store, say my good-byes as he sits in his cage, accept the cash from him, and then hit the road. No more helper monkeys! Maybe a cat this time?

THREE THINGS THAT YOU APPARENTLY CAN'T SAY IN AN OFFICE ENVIRONMENT

by Dan Kennedy

"I can take that project on with Steve. But I'll tell you . . . I don't want to do it. I'm having these weird feelings about everything lately. I have this anxiety thing where everything I do makes me feel uncomfortable. It's like the only thing I can even think about doing is staying in bed all day. Or fishing. I can handle fishing because you feel so close to God, you know?"

"I may be in late tomorrow; I've been doing this thing in the morning where I just stand in the shower and try to figure out what the hell I'm doing with my life. Just stand there for an hour going, 'Why am I even living in New York?' "

"I'm stepping out for some lunch. I have a weird feeling that I'm going to check into a hotel and try to forget about everything that my life has led to. Like, try to . . . kind of leave the old me behind and start my whole adult life over again. I think it's just a feeling, but if I don't come back today, and if I start to ignore your calls to my home . . . that's the deal. Because part of the unlearning everything will be acting like I don't know who you guys are."

NINE MUNDANE DREAMS

by Kevin Sampsell

1. You were in the laundry room and I walked in. You asked me what I wanted.

2. My mom was trying to grind some coffee beans, but the grinder wouldn't work. Then she realized it wasn't plugged in.

3. My grandfather was fishing at that really popular lake outside town. I drove up in a Ford Taurus and asked if he needed a ride home. He got in the car and farted.

4. My cat walked into the bedroom like he was going to make an announcement. I watched him for a couple minutes before I realized he couldn't talk.

5. I was at a Moby concert. He was fiddling with a keyboard and there were gospel singers shouting something over and over.

6. You were watching TV and I walked in and showed you the cable bill. I was wearing that hat I always wear.

7. I was reading this old biography of Gerald Ford when my neighbor knocked on the door. I answered it and he gave me back the hedge clippers I let him borrow.

8. My friend Matt was sitting on a ledge eating his lunch. At first I thought he was on a high building or bridge, but it was just a Safeway loading dock. He jumped off and walked away.

9. You were at a hockey game and that guy you slept with eight years ago was sitting a few rows away from you, closer to the ice. He looked the same, but maybe eight years older.

THINGS HEARD IN PROFESSOR VENKMAN'S COURSE LECTURES AT COLUMBIA UNIVERSITY BEFORE BEING TERMINATED BY THE BOARD OF REGENTS FOURTEEN MINUTES INTO *GHOSTBUSTERS*

by Martin Bell

"A number of you came up to me after class yesterday and asked me if it's possible to substitute the fourth edition of the text, *Introduction to Parapsychology,* for the fifth edition I listed on the syllabus. And of course, the answer is yes, provided you don't mind missing out on the entire chapter on past life aggression. Which, as it turns out, is 30 percent of what's on the final. So, yeah, save thirty bucks. Knock yourselves out."

"Hmmm . . . You know, this is kinda funny. Today, we have the technology to build an ecto-containment system for academic use, and yet none of us can get this damn slide projector working. Just hang—hang on a minute. Bear with us, guys."

"I'm not sure if the TAs made you aware of this, but I've canceled class tomorrow. I have to investigate an unexplained phenomenon at Shea Stadium. I'm told that it's seventeen to six with a point ninety-seven ERA over his last six starts. We'll do a makeup at some point."

"So, Egon and I finished grading your astral projection papers. The mean was around a B+, which is fine, but we wanted to show you guys something. See this? This is 'whose,' as in,

'Mr. Smith, *whose* wife died three years ago, has reported seeing her floating above his bed over a period of time coincident with the overall rise in psychokinetic energy.' And this is 'who's,' as in, '*Who's* going to tell me why nobody teaches you kids grammar in high school?' "

"Witnesses to this particular form of spirit photography often complain that the apparitions disappear—not unlike the secondary in the fourth quarter against Dartmouth last week, am I right? Ha-ha. Wait, nobody on the team's in this class, right?"

"Those of you who didn't bone up on the history of recorded telekinetic movement before the midterm, well, I'm sorry. But sometimes essay questions happen, and who ya gonna call?"

FABERGÉ'S LESSER-KNOWN WORKS

by Ed Page

Fabergé flapjack

Fabergé sausage link

Fabergé slice of bacon

Fabergé piece of toast

DAY JOBS OF YOUR LOCAL HAUNTED HOUSE EMPLOYEES

by Alysia Gray Painter

Evil Lumberjack will cash your check with two forms of ID

Dead Bride is pleased to neuter your cat for $10

Man in Hockey Mask is honored to serve your city as assistant mayor

Other Man in Hockey Mask sews for the local theater, joyfully

Fiendish Ghoul really enjoys making your vanilla malts

Cackling Mummy is a mommy-to-be

Mad Scientist watches television all day, wishes he'd stayed premed

Handsome Vampire scans want ads

Chain-Rattling Ghost haunts old train station rest of year, without chains

POORLY SUPPORTED CHARITIES

by John Moe

Habitrail for Humanity

International Kris Kross

People for the Ethical
Treatment of Assholes

Public Broadcasting System

Big Fat Brothers and Big
Mean Sisters

A PARTIAL LIST
OF NELL'S FAVORITE MOVIES

by Jonathan Shipley

T'ee an me an t'ee an me

Ressa

Chicka chickabee

SEEMED LIKE A GOOD IDEA AT THE TIME

by Beth Edwards

Wearing Avril Lavigne–style tie to mother's wedding

HIGHLIGHTS OF THE FIRST 100 DAYS OF A UNICORN PRESIDENT

by Margaret O'Leary

Universal health care

Simplification of tax code

Cancellation of stealth bomber program

Overhaul of campaign finance regulations

New laws to protect ancient forests

White House redecorated to look like eight-year-old girl's bedroom

UNSUITABLE CODE NAMES
FOR U.S. MILITARY OPERATIONS

by Jim Stallard

Swan Song   Shareholder Meeting

Ringworm   Awkward Silence

Reckless Impulse   Iraqi Freedom

Desert Sieve

MOST DISTURBING ORIFICES IN THE HEAD
TO BE BLEEDING FROM, ORDERED FROM
MOST DISTURBING TO LEAST DISTURBING

by Matthew Simmons

Ears

Eyes

Nose

Mouth

QUOTATIONS FROM "NO UGLY BABIES," A COMMUNITY THAT RATES THE CUTENESS OF APPLICANTS' BABIES

by Elizabeth Benefiel

"He's cute enough I guess."

"I didn't feel like there were really any good pictures and I'm pretty adamant about voting no for babies with their faces covered by pacifiers."

"As for cute factor, he just looks like a stereotypical baby."

"Yikes. I just lost my lunch."

"What the fuck happened to his head and what kind of crack were you smoking when you decided to take those awful pictures let alone post them on the INTRAWEB for millions to see? I suggest you do everything in your power to never ever have children again."

"I hope you die in a horrible, blazing fire."

"I have no nerves, I am nerveless."

"You think if some stranger calls me 'chink,' I shouldn't care? Do you think I can help caring?"

"Honestly, he looks a little retarded. Maybe it's just a stage."

"Oh and have you looked at your own baby lately? Chipmunk cheeks . . . *cringe*"

"I just read an interesting thread from a little over a month ago, and I had no idea that you were an anti-Semite. You really are a dumbass, aren't you?"

YOUR MOST INTIMATE
SEX QUESTIONS ANSWERED

by Mike Sacks

1. No.

2. No.

3. Sure, why not?

4. A coffee enema and a heaping slice of apple pie, piping hot, just out of the microwave, and then bed.

5. Yes, it is entirely acceptable to watch television with a lover while both strapped into a leather sex swing. But what should you watch? I can't really answer that, not being a qualified expert in television and all.

6. I wouldn't touch that if I were you.

7. Wouldn't touch that either, but that's just me.

8. Knees up, chest out, fingers spread, mouth agape, totally nude, riding by yourself in a convertible with the top down, silently mouthing the lyrics to "Maybe I'm Amazed."

9. Okay, okay, what do I care?

10. Wow. I've . . . that's a new one.

11. I'm gone. Find your own "answer man."

THINGS BOB SEGER DID "LIKE A ROCK" THAT, IN RETROSPECT, DO NOT SEEM ALL THAT ROCKLIKE

by Sean Carman

Felt like a million

Felt like number one

Worked for peanuts

Didn't have a care

Walked with purpose

Stood arrow straight

Stood proud

Stood tall

Believed in dreams

Charged from the gate

Carried the weight

YOU MIGHT BE A UNICORN IF

by Elizabeth Ellen

Your favorite color is sparkle.

Your family reunion consists of both horses and narwhals.

Your best friend is Rainbow Brite.

IDEAS FOR ANDY GOLDSWORTHY
SCULPTURES IN THE HOME

by Jordan Bass and Elizabeth Benefiel

Twig-pebble ziggurat erected
on cat's back; collapses when
cat wakes up

Large, ugly branches
conglomerated into large,
ugly branch sculpture in
living room; falls over when
inebriated teenage son walks
into it

Pillow fort

Stackable plastic chairs,
stacked on roof

Lawn cuttings carefully
distributed over lawn to give
lawn an ungroomed
appearance

METHODS OTHER THAN SONG
BY WHICH ONE CAN BE KILLED SOFTLY

by Jonathan Holley and Emily Lawton

Chinchilla attack

Asphyxiation by pound cake

Egyptian tomb booby-
trapped with goose down

Smothering by fatties

Poison meringue

Allergic reaction to cashmere

Stuffed-animal avalanche

Heart attack induced by
sixteen-year-old girl's skin

THREE METHODS FOR BEATING INSOMNIA
PASSED DOWN IN MY FAMILY

by Dan Kennedy

Long drive at night without
your glasses

Large tumbler of gin, review
financial regrets and
shortcomings

Diabetes

WAYS IN WHICH I HAVE PERSONALLY TAKEN IT UPON MYSELF TO MESS WITH TEXAS

by Beth Edwards

Took Texas's weekly
scheduling calendar off the
printer and said I didn't

Told Texas the lunch meeting
was at 1 P.M. instead of noon

Said I liked Texas's new
haircut when really one
sideburn was noticeably
longer than the other

Told Texas I really thought I
could see a relationship
between us, then stopped
returning Texas's phone calls

Acted like the seat next to
me at the bar was taken

Started rumor that I thought
I saw Texas out with Donna

Poured toner on Texas's chair